Estate Planning

101

and savvy

What The Wealthy ^ Do Differently

Sleep Every Night With Calm and Peace, Knowing Your Affairs Are In Order, Your Family, Charities, and Special Interests Are Taken Care of

Darryl Franklin, PhD

ISBN 978-0-9910007-2-2

Contents

PREFACE

When the inevitable happens, will you and your family be ready for it?

Everyone dies. It's a fact of life nobody can escape from, no matter how wealthy, powerful, or influential you are.

But while we know for sure that we *will* die, we can never know when, where, or how it will happen… and it could be sooner or more unexpected than you think.

When that happens, will your family be able to survive, let alone maintain their way of life, without you?

Without proper estate planning, you stand the risk of leaving your family in one heck of a tight spot – without money or the proper kind of care and support at a very traumatic time.

And even if you don't die, but become sick or incapacitated, will your family know and respect your wishes, making life-and-death decisions on your behalf? And can you afford the costs for the care needed without depleting your family's funds?

These are not things anyone likes to think about and it's easy to put off as something you will get around to one day… **But one day may come sooner than you think**.

That's why estate planning is so critical – whether you're a billionaire or an average Joe. It makes sure you **don't leave your family in the lurch** and ensures that you continue to support them even when you're no longer around.

This process may seem complicated and overwhelming – with so many considerations, paperwork, and legalities to manage. But it can be made easier with some fundamental knowledge about estate planning, possible help from an attorney, a financial planner, and/or tax professional, and this practical and easy-to-follow book.

Inside, you will discover:

- ✓ **How to best provide for and protect your loved ones after you're gone**, including your spouse, children, and any special causes close to your heart
- ✓ The unpleasant things you need to think about and prepare for today so you don't burden your family later on
- ✓ **The lowdown on death and taxes and how to minimize your tax obligations legally**
- ✓ How to protect your family from beyond the grave, and make sure squabbles over inheritance are kept to a minimum
- ✓ The secrets to **setting up a tank-like trust to shield you and your family** from a number of eventualities
- ✓ **What a real legacy can mean** – and how to leave behind a treasure of family traditions, life lessons, memories, and values for your family to cherish after you are gone

- ✓ **The pains of probate**, how to avoid this potentially lengthy process, and when it might be advantageous to go through it
- ✓ **Important documents you need to have in place before you die**, covering everything from end-of-life care to charitable contributions to inheritance.

And much more.

Taking smart and savvy steps to secure your family's future now will help you eliminate worry once and for all.

There's so much more to do than just having a will done. Cover all your bases and get a good night's sleep knowing you are ready no matter what comes!

INTRODUCTION

The most reliable way to predict the future is to create it

- Abraham Lincoln

Two different stories. Two different outcomes.

Two women, both in their 80s, both had achieved a level of financial success that many could only dream of. Each of these women, however, had taken a different approach to their wealth and estate planning. Their journeys offer valuable insights into the true meaning of success and the role that our resources play in our lives.

CONTENTMENT IN SIMPLICITY

The first woman, a single, retired math teacher, lived in a humble ranch-style home. Her cozy abode, filled with mismatched furniture and personal mementos, exuded warmth and kindness. Throughout her life, she had worked in one of the most challenging schools in the city, sharing her love and passion for teaching with her students.

Unbeknownst to many, this woman had become wealthy with disciplined investing having grown her wealth through careful but regular investments in equities via Wall Street and her personal real estate. When the time came to create her life estate plan, she gave generously to those she cared for and her church. Her wealth did not define her; she lived a life of love, generosity, and purpose, anchored firmly in her faith.

FEAR AND INSECURITY

The second woman, a widow with an estate worth over $20 million, faced a vastly different situation. Her children, having already inherited substantial wealth from their father and having achieved success in their careers, did not need any inheritance from their mother. They encouraged her to give to charity, avoid significant estate taxes, and experience the joy of philanthropy.

Despite assurance from financial advisors that she would be secure even if she gave away a substantial portion of her estate, this woman could not overcome her fear of running out of money. She chose not to give, and in the end, a large portion of her estate was lost to taxes. Instead of providing her freedom and peace, her wealth brought her constant worry and insecurity.

A LESSON IN HEART AND PERSPECTIVE

These two women and their contrasting experiences help illuminate that the choice to give or keep is ultimately a matter of the heart. It is not about how much wealth one has but rather the role one allows their financial resources to play. True success is not found in accumulating assets or maintaining a certain lifestyle but in understanding that our identity and security should not be tied to our wealth. I believe it should be about "living our best life."

One of your fears may be the possibility of family disputes over inheritance, which can damage relationships among your loved ones. You also care deeply about the welfare of your minor or special needs children and grandchildren, and you want to ensure they continue receiving the support they need once you are no longer living.

You may very well have thoughts of your well-being in the event of disability, incapacitation, or illness as you age. You want to ensure that your estate is well managed and that you are adequately cared for during potentially challenging times.

Leaving a lasting legacy is important to you. You want to be remembered as someone who positively impacted the world and lived a meaningful life. Passing on a set of values and ideas that will be cherished by your family, friends, and loved ones for years to come is the icing on the cake.

I get it—these are the types of concerns and wishes I hear regularly from our client review meetings. I've written this book to provide a roadmap to guide you through the estate planning process, helping you address these pain points and action steps to achieve the peace of mind you deserve. You'll find practical, easy-to-follow advice on creating a well-rounded estate plan that considers your unique situation and goals, ultimately giving you the confidence to focus on what truly matters: enjoying your later years and living a "worry-free," comfortable lifestyle.

This book provides the tools and knowledge to create a comprehensive estate plan that addresses your unique needs and circumstances.

Together, we will explore dozens of options, concerns, and considerations for a great estate plan. We'll learn from the experiences of others and identify the best strategies for your specific situation. You'll use the insight from this book to develop a plan of action to ensure that your affairs are in order and that you can sleep soundly at night, knowing that you've done everything in your power to provide for those who matter most to you.

This book will guide you through the process and provide valuable insights into what the wealthy and savvy do differently regarding estate planning. Here are a few benefits you'll gain from reading this book:

1. Simplified Estate Planning: No more feeling overwhelmed by legal jargon and complex concepts. You'll learn practical, clear, and easy-to-follow guidelines to help you create a comprehensive estate plan tailored to your unique circumstances.
2. Minimized Family Conflict: You'll discover strategies to prevent potential family disputes after you're gone by clearly outlining who gets what, reducing the chances of misunderstandings, arguments, and heaven forbid, forever damaged relationships.
3. Protection for Minor or Special Needs Dependents: This book will help you explore options for ensuring that your minor or special needs children or grandchildren are well cared for when you are no longer present.

4. Planning for Incapacity: Learn how to create a plan that addresses what will happen if you become disabled, incapacitated, or unable to advocate for yourself due to old age or illness, e.g., Alzheimer's, Parkinson's, etc.

5. Leaving a Lasting Legacy: You will discover how to create a legacy that reflects your values and ideas, ensuring that you are remembered as someone who positively impacts life, your family, and the world.

Reading this book and implementing the strategies outlined within, you'll be able to focus on what truly matters - enjoying your later years, spending quality time with your family/friends, and pursuing your passions.

This book results from countless hours of study, research, and practical, day-to-day experiences with clients to help them live their best lives where "estate planning" is one of five pillars required to accomplish a "worry-free" comfortable lifestyle. This book is the aftereffect of the wonderful "work" I am privileged to do daily, helping clients, and sharing secrets that the wealthy and savvy do differently.

When you finish reading, you'll understand the estate planning process and know how to tailor it specifically for your unique situation.

You'll have a clear roadmap for navigating the complexities of estate and trust laws and a solid grasp of the tax implications associated with your estate. With this knowledge, you can confidently create a plan that maximizes the value of your assets while minimizing tax liabilities for your beneficiaries.

Moreover, you'll have the tools to create a lasting legacy that reflects your values and supports the causes closest to your heart. Your friends, family, and future generations will remember you as someone who achieved financial success and used that success to make a meaningful and lasting impact on the world.

In short, by reading this book and implementing its guidance, you can expect to achieve:

1. Confidence in navigating the often-complex nature of estate planning and tax laws.
2. A clear and practical plan to distribute your assets according to your wishes.
3. Success strategies to minimize tax liabilities and maximize the value of your estate.
4. An enhanced process for developing a lasting legacy that reflects your values and positively impacts the people you love.

As a financial expert with a background in both the academic and practical aspects of finance, I have dedicated the "back nine of my life" to helping individuals like you make informed decisions about their financial futures. My unique blend of faith, finance, education, and experience provides a particular perspective not available anywhere else.

As a trained theologian and an ordained clergyman, my life is faith-focused. I start each day by reading my Bible. I have found that starting each day this way helps to set the tone for the day and centers me. Let me highlight a piece of ancient wisdom found in the fourth chapter of Philippians, where the apostle Paul writes, "The secret to contentment in all circumstances is found in Christ, who provides us with strength and purpose." The pastor in me interprets this to mean, "When we recognize that everything we have is a gift from God, meant to be stewarded for God's purposes, we can live lives of generosity, joy, and true success." The theologian in me heralds the belief that we must examine our hearts and consider where we place our hope and security - and how best to live our best life.

Let's get started.

PART 1: TANGIBLE WEALTH

CHAPTER ONE

DISCIPLINE NOW OR CHAOS LATER…

Discipline is the bridge between goals and accomplishment.

- Jim Rohn

WHAT IS ESTATE PLANNING?

Estate planning is crucial to managing your financial life, ensuring that your hard-earned assets and wealth are correctly handled and distributed according to your wishes. It involves making decisions and arrangements for managing and distributing your assets and liabilities after your death or mental/physical incapacitation.

At its core, estate planning is about taking control of your financial legacy and providing for the well-being of your loved ones and special interests. A well-crafted estate plan ensures that your wealth, assets, and income are distributed according to your wishes and helps minimize taxes, fees, and other legal complications that can arise during the distribution process.

Some key components of estate planning include:

1. Drafting Your Will and Last Testament: Your will and last testament are powerful documents. This binding contract communicates your desires for asset distribution and the safekeeping of any young ones upon your passing.
2. Forming a Trust Agreement: A Trust Agreement is a unique legal framework that endows a selected third party - known as the trustee - with the authority to retain and supervise assets for the recipient's benefit. Trusts offer a flexible and sophisticated means to cater to your specific needs.
3. Trusts can effectively manage and protect your assets, both during your lifetime and after your death. They can provide financial stability and privacy to help avoid the often lengthy and costly probate process.
4. Naming Beneficiaries: Designating beneficiaries for your various assets without the probate process.
5. Assigning powers of attorney: If you can't make these decisions for yourself, you appoint somebody to decide financially and healthcare-wise on your behalf.
6. Planning for taxes and other expenses: Proper estate planning will help minimize the tax burden on your estate, ensuring that your beneficiaries receive the maximum amount of your assets.
7. Addressing unique family situations: Estate planning allows you to provide for family members with special needs, protect your assets from potential creditors, and address other unique family dynamics and concerns.

In the following chapters, we will unpack dozens of estate planning components to provide the guidance you need to create a well-rounded estate plan tailored to your needs and desires.

WHY IS IT A GOOD IDEA?

Reflecting on the statistical data gathered in 2020 by Gallup, it was revealed that just under half, precisely 46%, of American adults had formally laid out their wishes in a Last Testament, dictating the future management of their financial assets and estates posthumously. This percentage remains remarkably consistent, echoing the findings of three previous studies conducted on this matter since the dawn of the 1990s.

Estate planning is an essential process that benefits almost everyone regardless of their net worth. Let's explore some of the key reasons as to why estate planning is a good idea:

- Control Over Asset Distribution: A well-crafted estate plan eliminates the potential for misunderstandings or disputes among family members. It prevents your estate from being distributed according to the state's default rules, which likely would not align with your intentions.
- Minimizing Taxes and Expenses: Proper estate planning can help reduce the taxes and expenses of transferring assets to your beneficiaries. This includes reducing estate taxes, capital gains taxes, and probate expenses.
- Financial Security for Loved Ones: An estate plan will enable you to provide financial security for your spouse, children, grandchildren, and other beneficiaries. You can establish trusts, designate beneficiaries for retirement accounts and life insurance policies, and create plans to provide ongoing support

for loved ones with special needs or other unique circumstances.

- Appointment of Healthcare and Financial Decision-Makers: Estate planning is about distributing your assets and planning for your well-being.

Estate planning is a necessary process allowing you to take control of your financial legacy, provide for your loved ones, and ensure your well-being. By engaging in estate planning, you can sleep each night with calm and peace, knowing that your affairs are in order and that the gift of your life will positively impact your family, charities, and special interests. So, let's start creating a comprehensive estate plan tailored to your unique needs and desires.

WHERE DO I START?

Starting your estate planning journey begins with clearly understanding your assets and liabilities. Follow these steps to create an organized and comprehensive asset inventory:

1. Gather Financial Documents

Start by collecting all financial documents, including bank statements, investment portfolios, property deeds, mortgage documents, insurance policies, and retirement account statements. These documents will help you compile an accurate and up-to-date list of your assets and liabilities.

2. List Your Assets

Create a comprehensive list of your assets, including:

- ✓ Properties under your ownership in the real estate realm
- ✓ Banking profiles, including checking and savings accounts

- ✓ Investment portfolios containing stocks, bonds, and mutual funds
- ✓ Retirement reservoirs
- ✓ Life insurance contracts
- ✓ Valuable personal property (artwork, jewelry, collectibles)
- ✓ Vehicles (cars, boats, motorcycles)
- ✓ Business interests or partnerships

For each asset, record important details such as the current market value, account numbers, and ownership information (sole or joint ownership).

3. List Your Liabilities

Next, compile a list of your outstanding debts and liabilities, such as

- ✓ Home loans, otherwise known as mortgages
- ✓ Auto financing arrangements
- ✓ Personal borrowing commitments
- ✓ Outstanding balances on credit cards
- ✓ Medical debts
- ✓ Taxes owed

Include important information such as the outstanding balance, interest rate, monthly payment, and loan terms.

4. Organize Your Information

Organize your asset and liability information logically, using a spreadsheet or a dedicated financial software program. This will make reviewing your financial situation more manageable and allow you to update the information as needed.

5. Update Regularly

Regularly update your asset inventory to ensure that it remains accurate and reflects any changes in your financial situation. This update process should include the acquisition or sale of assets, changes in account balances, or fluctuations in the value of investments.

6. Share Your Inventory with Trusted Individuals

Share your asset inventory with trusted family members, your attorney, or your financial advisor, ensuring they have access to this vital information in the event of your incapacitation or death.

With a comprehensive understanding of your assets and liabilities, you can make informed decisions about distributing your wealth and protecting your loved ones' financial future. Ultimately, this process will provide you with greater peace of mind as you work toward ensuring your affairs are in order and your legacy is secure.

TO WHOM DO I WANT TO INHERIT MY ASSETS?

Deciding who will inherit your estate (i.e. beneficiary) is a personal and meaningful choice.

Consider your unique circumstances and preferences as you think about your estate plan. These may include family structure, relationships with friends and family, financial situation, charitable giving, and values. By carefully considering these factors, you can make informed decisions about who should inherit your estate and how it should be distributed.

Some factors to consider when making these decisions include:

- Your family structure: Do you have a spouse, children, or other dependents you want to provide for?

- Your relationships: Do you have close relationships with certain family members or friends that you want to include in your estate plan?
- Financial considerations: Do you have debts or obligations to pay off, or do you want to minimize taxes for your heirs?
- Charitable giving: Do you want to leave some of your assets to charitable organizations?
- Your values: Do you have specific values or beliefs that you want to reflect in your estate plan, such as supporting education or promoting environmental sustainability?

When choosing beneficiaries, it's essential to consider what might happen if your primary beneficiary(ies) passes away before you.

Remember, you can constantly update your will if your circumstances change or if you want to make any adjustments. Keeping your estate plan updated should be part of a fiscal planning and management routine.

With your affairs in order, you can sleep every night with calmness and peace, knowing that you're leaving the world a better place and that your life has genuinely mattered.

APPOINTING AN EXECUTOR(S)

Selecting the right individuals to handle your affairs when you can no longer do so is critical. In this section, I'll discuss the importance of appointing a trusted executor and having power of attorney to ensure your healthcare and financial decisions are made according to your wishes.

An executor(s) is responsible for administering your estate after your passing. They will be in charge of tasks such as paying off any outstanding debts, distributing assets according to your will, and filing tax returns on behalf of your estate. It's essential to choose someone you trust to act in the best interests of your beneficiaries and carry out your wishes. Side note: I've seen instances where two people are named as the executor. While this looks good on paper, especially if you have two children and name them both as executors, this can lead to indecision if the parties can not agree on a single avenue of action. My two cents is to pick one person and then name a successor executor if the first person fails to execute your wishes appropriately. Yes, you'll be gone, and it won't matter to you then, but if the goal is for your wishes to be carried out with minimal mishaps, then I suggest having only one named executor. Pick wisely!

When selecting an executor, consider the following factors:

1. Trustworthiness: Your executor should be someone you have complete confidence in to handle your financial affairs with honesty and integrity.
2. Organizational skills: Managing an estate can involve various tasks, paperwork, and deadlines. Your executor should be well-organized and detail-oriented.
3. Availability and willingness: Your executor should have time availability and a heart to help you complete your estate.
4. Familiarity with your wishes: Securing someone invested in your thoughts, desires, and demeanor will be a bonus for your estate plan

Power of Attorney for Healthcare and Finances

A power of attorney - let's call it a POA for short - serves as your lifeline in challenging times. This official piece of paperwork hands over the baton of decision-making to a trusted individual of your choice should a situation arise where you cannot call the shots. The unpredictable nature of life may render you incapacitated or leave you in a state where decision-making becomes a mountain too high to climb. And that's precisely where a POA steps in, ensuring that someone you trust implicitly is at the helm, guiding your affairs in your stead.

There are two types of POA you should consider:

1. Healthcare POA: This person will make medical decisions for you if you cannot do so. They should clearly understand your values, beliefs, and medical preferences.
2. Financial POA: This individual will manage your financial affairs, including paying bills, managing investments, and making other financial decisions if you cannot do so.

When choosing a POA, consider the following:

1. Trustworthiness: Like your executor, your POA should be someone you trust to make decisions that align with your best interests.
2. Knowledge of your preferences: Your POA should know your values and desires, especially regarding healthcare and financial matters.
3. Availability and willingness: Your POA should have time availability and a heart to help you complete your estate.

Do-It-Yourself, Attorney, or Hybrid

Every dollar was important to me as a young man starting out in life with a young family. Consequently, I became very handy with home repairs and decor updates. I was willing to try just about everything first before calling a professional. As I have matured and realize that I likely have less time ahead of me than behind me, time has become more valuable to me than money. By that, I mean I would much rather spend time with family or enjoy time with friends than do lawn maintenance or paint a room. It is much easier to send an email, have someone show up to do the work professionally and have it done right the first time. This is especially true on big projects like bath remodels or roof installations.

In like fashion, I know some people will use this book to aid them in creating their estate plans themselves. In that case, do-it-yourself estate planning is a valid option. There are a number of online sites to help you; for example, LegalZoom.com and NOLO.com immediately come to mind.

Suppose you have a large estate or complicated issues such as a second or third marriage, special needs children, etc. In that case, I urge you to think of your estate plan as completing a bath remodel or putting on a new roof as a rookie handyman… yes, you probably could do it, but would it reflect the best possible outcome?

Time for most of my clients is more valuable than money, and paying someone to complete the estate plan and have it done right the first time is a much better alternative than do-it-yourself.

Hiring an estate attorney versed in tax and law greatly benefits ensuring your wishes are carried out, and taxes are minimized.

Hiring an estate planning attorney may sound like a colossal task, but let's face it: It's a decision that will hold enormous importance in the long run. And believe me, with the proper research and an open mind, it can be one of the best decisions you've ever made. Here's what you need to watch for:

1. Experience: We've all heard the saying, "Practice makes perfect." It holds especially true in the field of estate planning. Look for an attorney who has significant experience in this area. The pros of hiring an experienced attorney are manifold; they can easily navigate the legal complexities, help you avoid common pitfalls, and tailor a plan to fit your unique needs and wishes. The only potential downside could be the costs of hiring a seasoned professional, but with an estate with multiple variables, it may very well be a worthy investment.
2. Specialization: Estate planning is a broad field with various subcategories such as trust administration, probate, elder law, tax planning, and more. The “pros” of hiring an attorney specializing in estate planning are that they will be fully aware of the ins and outs of this area, including the latest laws and regulations. However, the cons may include not being versatile enough to handle legal issues outside their expertise. So, pick an attorney who suits your particular situation best.
3. Reputation: What others say about an attorney can give you critical insight. Positive testimonials and reviews reflect the attorney's competence and professionalism. You may want to steer clear if you notice red flags or consistent complaints. The downside? Well, reviews can sometimes be misleading or

manipulated. Therefore, while relying on reviews, always consider the bigger picture and do your due diligence.

4. Communication: Estate planning involves handling some of your life's most personal and significant aspects. If you hire an attorney, you'll want one who communicates clearly, listens attentively, and respects your input. The advantage of having a communicative attorney is that you'll always be in the loop and feel a part of the process. The only potential con might be that such a relationship may take time to develop.
5. Fees: Transparency in the fee structure is crucial to avoid any unpleasant surprises later. Weigh the pros of the services provided against the costs. Although some might find the attorney's fees intimidating, remember, the investment you make now in quality legal advice can save you and your heirs a significant amount of money and distress in the future.

Of course, every decision comes with potential downsides, and hiring an estate planning attorney is no exception. Understanding both sides of the coin is crucial to make an informed decision. Here are some potential cons:

1. The expense factor: It is true… Hiring legal counsel can be costly. Think of it as an investment that provides a high return in the long haul. Please don't shy away from hiring an experienced, well-educated lawyer; they can effectively pay for themselves by getting it done right the first time. Yes, it's a fact that you could scribble down some rudimentary documents

using the plethora of online tools available, but let's not forget that estate planning is a maze that's not so easy to navigate. Even a minor blunder could spawn a series of significant complications in the future. Hence, shelling out for an attorney might seem like you're parting with your hard-earned money, but consider this an investment that could keep your bank balance in the green in the long run.

2. Overly complex: When you hire an attorney, especially a very thorough one, you might end up with a more complex estate plan than necessary. An overcomplicated plan could be complicated for your heirs to navigate, potentially leading to disputes or confusion. It's essential to balance having a comprehensive plan and keeping it straightforward enough for everyone involved to understand.
3. Impersonality: Lawyers, given the nature of their work, can sometimes be seen as distant or unemotional. This can make discussing personal matters, like estate planning, somewhat uncomfortable.
4. Time-consuming: Creating an effective estate plan can be time-consuming. An attorney will need to know your financial situation, family structure, wishes, and more. This is a process that can't be rushed. Some may view this as a negative, especially if they're looking for a quick solution.
5. Difficulties in finding the right match: Finding an attorney who meets your needs, understands your situation, and communicates effectively can be challenging. It might take a

meeting with several attorneys before you find the right one, which can be frustrating.

These potential cons aren't meant to dissuade you from hiring an estate planning attorney but rather to encourage you to consider all aspects before making a decision.

Other Legal Documents

An attorney can help you create other essential legal documents, including:

1. Advance Healthcare Directive: This document outlines your preferences for medical care if incapacitated.
2. Beneficiary Designations: These designations ensure that your retirement accounts are distributed according to your wishes.
3. Letter of Instruction: Although not legally binding, a letter of intent guides your executor or trustee regarding your wishes and values.

GETTING "AROUNDTOIT"

Face it…Like most people, you probably didn't wake up this morning eager to finally start and complete your estate planning. Many know they should have their estate plan done but put it off, expecting to do the work when they get "aroundtoit."

Look at 12 common reasons people procrastinate about their estate plan and suggestions on overcoming these obstacles.

1. Facing mortality and money: Feeling uneasy about discussing death and finances is normal. However, facing these issues

head-on will provide your loved ones peace of mind and security.

2. Lack of a deadline: Although there's no specific deadline for estate planning, it's essential to recognize that it's an ongoing responsibility that should be revisited periodically.
3. Estate planning isn't fun: While it may not be the most exciting task, focusing on the benefits for your family and legacy can make the process more fulfilling.
4. Lawyers can be expensive: True, but so is completing the plan incorrectly or missing key tax provisions, exemptions, or deadlines. Investing in professional guidance now can save your estate from costly mistakes.
5. Fear of paperwork: Break down the process into manageable steps and ask for help from a knowledgeable professional to clarify any confusing aspects.
6. Not reaping the benefits personally: Embrace the satisfaction of knowing you are securing your loved ones' future.
7. Potential conflict within the family: Communicate openly with your family members and explain your decisions to minimize misunderstandings.
8. Overwhelmed by the task: Tackle estate planning one step at a time, focusing on the most critical elements first.
9. Passive-aggressive behavior: Prioritize your loved ones' well-being and address any unresolved issues separately.
10. Living in the moment: Balance short-term pleasure with long-term planning to achieve lasting peace of mind.

11. Seeking perfection: Focus on your overall wishes and understand that no estate plan will cover every possible scenario.
12. Guilt from procrastination: Recognize that taking action now is better than never addressing your estate planning needs. Accountability can be found by hiring a professional to help guide you and ensure you get it done.

Estate planning may be challenging, but the benefits far outweigh the discomfort. Addressing these common reasons for procrastination and acting can ensure a more secure future for your loved ones and leave a lasting legacy.

If you're not disciplined and dislike administration, estate planning may seem overwhelming. However, the most important thing is to ACT…here are three steps you can take to simplify the process and make it more manageable:

1. Start with the basics: Create a simple will and appoint a healthcare proxy and power of attorney.
2. Use technology: Many online tools and apps, such as legal document templates, digital organization tools, and online calculators, help simplify estate planning.
3. Take it one step at a time: Don't try to tackle everything at once. Break the process down into manageable steps and set achievable goals for yourself.

Remember that estate planning is essential to your future and your loved ones' security.

"Oh My Goodness" Stories…

Estate planning is the power to continue making an impact long after you are gone. Ideally, that impact should be positive. If not done well, a poorly executed or neglected plan can leave your loved ones grappling with financial and legal challenges, making the grieving process even more difficult.

The Disappearing Documents

Essential estate planning documents, i.e., a will and trust, clarify your intentions and provide a roadmap for asset distribution. When these documents are missing or incomplete, your family may face a nightmare of a legal journey.

When the acclaimed media figure Larry King passed in 2021, he left behind an estate valued at $2 million, with a significant additional wealth held in trust, tallying up to many millions more. Despite his substantial wealth, King's passing ignited a complex legal dispute over his will due to the incomplete formal documentation of his estate plans. This story underscores questions about the benefits and complexities of estate and trust management, underscoring the importance of precise legal planning in preserving one's wealth and ensuring a smooth transition of assets.

1. Who should administer the estate? Larry King Jr., the eldest surviving child, claimed responsibility, but no written evidence supported his claim.

2. How should the inheritance be divided? Two of King's children had died after he wrote the will, leaving the distribution of their share unclear.
3. What about King's soon-to-be ex-wife? King was in the process of divorcing Shawn King, who was named as the executor in his 2015 will. Shawn contested the validity of the 2019 will, arguing that King was not mentally competent when he wrote it.

The ensuing legal battle between the wife and the eldest son would last years and consume a significant portion of the estate.

Hollywood Drama of John Singleton

Acclaimed Hollywood filmmaker John Singleton slipped into a coma in April 2019. As his family grappled with this unexpected turn of events, they discovered that Singleton had not prepared a medical directive or power of attorney in case of incapacity, leading to a bitter battle over guardianship.

Singleton's death 13 days later revealed another unsettling discovery: his last will, created in 1993, had never been updated. At the time, he had only one daughter. Over the following 26 years, Singleton fathered at least four other children, with two additional children potentially his. Unfortunately, his will did not account for these new, by blood, family members.

Singleton reportedly had a net worth of approximately $35 million at the time of his death but left behind an estate valued considerably less at $3.8 million. This disparity led to conjecture that the rest of his wealth might be tied up in a trust. Despite these speculations, the likelihood of this scenario seems slim, considering it would be highly unconventional for someone to establish a trust and simultaneously not create or amend a will into a 'pour-over' will, which could lead to familial discord and emotional distress as legal disputes surface. This is precisely what happened in the aftermath. Better planning with an intentional focus on his lifestyle and interests would have helped prevent conflict and saved thousands in legal fees, court costs, and the emotional distress of his surviving family members.

Famed Actor James Gandolfini

Remember James Gandolfini? That stellar actor whose legacy continues to shine. Most recognized for breathing life into the character Tony Soprano on HBO's much-lauded series, *The Sopranos*, Gandolfini's performance remains unforgettable. He left behind an enduring legacy in television and an estate valued at an estimated $70 million. However, the handling of his estate provides crucial lessons for those interested in estate planning.

Drafted in 2012, Gandolfini's will was a relatively simple document that divided his estate among his sisters, wife, and two children. While it's commendable that Gandolfini took steps to ensure his wishes were outlined, the structure of his will led to several complications.

The Problems

1. Lack of Privacy: Gandolfini's will was admitted to probate, a public process. This meant the details of his estate, including the recipients and the amounts they received, became public knowledge. An estate

planning expert could have advised Gandolfini on strategies to keep his estate private, like establishing trusts.

2. Estate Taxes: A significant portion of Gandolfini's estate was subject to hefty estate taxes. His will stipulated that the shares of his sisters and infant daughter were to be paid outright rather than placed in trust. As a result, about $30 million of his estate was lost to taxes. A proficient estate planning attorney and/or tax professional could have employed strategies to minimize estate tax implications.

3. Minor Children's Inheritance: Gandolfini's son would receive his portion of the inheritance outright at age 21. Most estate planning experts advise against such arrangements, as young adults may be unprepared to responsibly handle large sums of money. Trusts could be structured to distribute assets over time or when the child reaches a more mature age.

The Lessons

The issues surrounding Gandolfini's estate underscore the importance of robust estate planning with the guidance of an expert.

1. Minimize Estate Taxes: Estate planning experts can advise and implement strategies to minimize estate taxes, ensuring more of your wealth goes to your heirs rather than taxes. This could include using certain types of trusts or gifting strategies during your lifetime.

2. Protect Your Privacy: A well-drafted estate plan can help maintain your family's privacy after your passing.

3. Careful Planning for Minor Children: An estate planning expert can help you craft a plan that not only provides for your minor children

but also safeguards them from the potential pitfalls of receiving a large inheritance at a young age. This might involve creating trusts that dispense assets over time or under specific circumstances.

It's not enough to have a will; you need an expertly crafted estate plan that protects your assets, your privacy, and the interests of your heirs. Your legacy is too important to leave to chance.

A Cautionary Tale: Egelhoff v. Egelhoff

David and Donna Rae Egelhoff were an unhappy couple who decided to divorce. Merely two months after finalizing their divorce, David tragically died in a car accident, leaving behind a life insurance policy and a pension plan. Although he had two children from a previous marriage, he neglected to designate them as beneficiaries following his divorce.

His children sued for the money but ultimately lost the case, leaving the inheritance to the now-former ex-spouse, and his children were burdened with plenty of new and unnecessary legal costs.

The Unfunded Trust: A Harrowing Account

Consider this chilling tale a law firm shares involving clients who set up a trust. They transferred their real estate and assigned their LLC correctly, but tragically, they never completed the necessary account ownership and beneficiary change forms.

When the clients passed away, the assets remained in their names rather than in the trust, exposing the estate to probate and leaving their son with an unfunded trust. Grieving the loss of his parents, the son also faced a lengthy and unexpected probate process. To add to the misery, the son might now have to pay an estate tax, which could have been reduced or avoided altogether if the trust had been properly funded.

CHAPTER SUMMARY

Ensuring a comfortable lifestyle in the latter part of life is a top planning priority. For most, having a positive impact on others or the larger community after they are no longer living is a priority for proactive estate planning.

As you approach or find yourself already experiencing a comfortable lifestyle in the later stages of life, regardless of whether you've officially "retired" or not, it's crucial to prioritize estate planning. Your decisions will significantly impact your financial security, your loved ones, and the causes you care about in the future.

Retirement planning is integral to estate planning, as it sets the foundation for managing your assets, protecting your family, and leaving a lasting legacy.

Later in Chapter 7, *Shielding & Sheltering Your Wealth*, we'll delve deeper into the critical components of retirement planning, including:

1. Assessing your financial situation: Understanding your current net worth and expenses will give you a clear picture of your financial health as you retire.
2. Setting retirement goals: Identifying your financial goals and lifestyle desires for retirement will help guide your estate planning decisions and ensure you have the resources to enjoy the life you've always envisioned.

3. Developing an investment strategy: Develop a custom investment strategy that aligns with your risk tolerance, time horizon, and financial objectives will help you build and preserve your wealth in retirement.
4. Planning for healthcare and long-term care: Considering potential healthcare expenses and long-term care needs is crucial for protecting your assets.
5. Managing taxes and estate planning laws: Staying informed about tax laws and estate planning regulations will allow you to make informed decisions that minimize tax liabilities and protect your estate.
6. Creating a legacy plan: Establishing a plan to pass on your values, ideas, and wealth to future generations and charitable causes will ensure that your life's impact lasts for decades and, if done well, for generations to come.

To be clear, your retirement planning and estate planning efforts are unique to you. Your goals, priorities, and personal circumstances will shape your path, and this book will help guide and motivate you to complete your estate plan, taking advantage of best practices we've seen and helping others execute to complete their custom, personalized estate plans.

CHAPTER TWO

LAWSUITS AND LEGAL EAGLES

We educated, privileged lawyers have a professional and moral duty to represent the underrepresented in our society and ensure that justice exists for all, both legal and economic.

- Sonia Sotomayor, U.S. Supreme Court Justice

CHOOSING AN ATTORNEY…

Navigating the labyrinth of estate planning is no cakewalk, and professional guidance often proves to be the lifeline. However, not everyone can afford the price of a legal eagle. That's where legal aid steps up to the plate. These nonprofit organizations offer gratis legal aid to folks who can't foot the bill for a lawyer. Primarily designed for those with severely restricted incomes, some offices offer a little leeway on the income restrictions and present self-help resources for a jump-start on estate planning.

These legal aid bureaus deal with many issues - immigration, consumer matters, disability-related issues, and more. Some may specialize in particular legal areas, such as housing or disability.

However, it's worth noting that government funding might put a leash on the types of cases they can entertain.

Hunting for a local legal aid office? Look no further than www.LawHelp.org. Just click on the state you live in, and voila! You can find out who can assist with your legal hiccup within your state.

There are areas where legal aid might have to pass, such as civil legal aid, which doesn't extend to cases concerning monetary damages, including medical malpractice, vehicle accident scenarios, traffic violation cases, or criminal cases. Rest assured, legal aid lawyers are every bit as qualified as their counterparts, and your discussions with them will always remain confidential.

If the scope of legal aid doesn't encompass your legal issue, consider contacting your local bar association. They can connect you with a private attorney specializing in your legal issue, who might be open to consultation at a reduced fee.

Wondering about alternate sources of assistance? Here are some options:

The American Bar Association's Free Legal Answers program: This innovative online platform connects needy individuals with volunteer attorneys. These professionals offer their expertise at no cost, providing swift responses to legal queries online.

State Court System's Self-help centers: These hubs offer various complimentary services, such as workshops, educational materials, court forms, and assistance with form completion.

Local Law Schools: These institutions often operate free legal clinics where law students, under the guidance of their professors, offer free legal aid.

Local Area Agency on Aging: This agency is designed to support seniors (60 years and older) with a range of issues, including providing free or low-cost legal help.

Consider Mary, a 60-year-old woman who, after a health scare, is at her wit's end about her estate planning. Mary knows her budget is tight, and hiring a lawyer this month is unrealistic. Undeterred, she makes a beeline for her local legal aid office, and they guide her on will creation, trust setup, and beneficiary designation for her life insurance policy. Mary breathes a sigh of relief, knowing her estate will be handled as she desires, ensuring her loved ones are cared for after she passes on.

WHAT TO KNOW BEFORE YOU CALL AN ATTORNEY

Tackling a legal quandary? Then, tracking down the right attorney is your top priority. Picking an attorney should mirror the selection of an accountant or a contractor, executed with thoughtfulness and due diligence. You'll be entrusting them with confidential information and relying on their advice to make the best possible plan of action that might otherwise leave you floundering and potentially legally exposed, with your ultimate wishes never fully materializing.

Deciding on the finest legal eagle involves weighing several factors, from credentials and cost to specialization, location, and compatibility.

Long or Short-Term Representation: Start your search by carefully identifying your needs. What's your reason for needing an attorney? What's the legal pickle you're caught up in? Once you discern the need for legal aid, decide if it's a fleeting or sustained requirement. A one-off consultation might do the trick if you need advice on a pressing legal issue. But if you're looking for a legal luminary to handle all your legal matters indefinitely, you're better off with an experienced attorney who gels with your personality.

Area of Law: Much like doctors have their medical specialties, lawyers, too, have their preferred legal field. Pinpoint the area your situation falls under and scout for an expert attorney. Naturally, an estate planning whizz should be preferred over your friend, who is a generalist but primarily handles real estate transactions.

Reputation: You want an attorney who knows their stuff and has a track record to prove it. Don't shy away from seeking recommendations from folks who have collaborated with the attorney in the past or tap into online referral services to track down a certified lawyer in your locality.

Location: Laws differ from one state to another, making it essential to find an attorney well-versed in the legal nuances in your area. Those living in rural zones with sparse resources may find phone or email consultations adequate for minor issues. But when dealing with heftier legal matters or long-term advice, proximity is critical to building a trusted, personal rapport. Please don't shy away from virtual meetings in our post-COVID world. They greatly enhance a relationship when time, distance, and convenience are at a premium.

Experience: Choose an attorney who enjoys estate planning work. A little sleuthing can help uncover their practice history – either send them a question or visit their firm's website. While experience is a prized asset, ensure it aligns with your situation and budget.

Size of Firm: The size of the firm is another deciding factor. Big fish might be more established and resource-rich, but their services come at a higher price. Small boutique firms often offer a more intimate experience at a friendlier price but might fall short if they don't cater to your specific area of law.

Cost and Billing: Gauge your ability to spend on legal representation. Ask the attorney for an estimate and learn about their billing system. This could be hourly charges, fixed rates, contingency fees, negotiable fees, or retainers for future charges. Ensure you understand any additional expenses like shipping, filing, and travel, as these could be billed separately.

Compatibility: Look beyond professional qualifications to assess the attorney's personality. Pick someone you trust, who treats you respectfully, and who you can be comfortable with. A diligent attorney with good judgment and communication skills is an invaluable ally.

Availability: Ensure the attorney you're eyeing has enough capacity to devote to your case. If they appear swamped or can't take up your work for weeks, you might have to find someone who can promptly cater to your needs.

When it comes to estate planning – a critical task of managing and distributing your assets after your passing – it's imperative to find an attorney who's adept in estate planning and someone you're comfortable confiding personal details. Consider the following questions and factors to find the right estate planning attorney.

Finding the right lawyer for your trust fund

Consider the following steps and factors to find the best lawyer for your trust fund.

1. Seek Referrals: Ask family, friends, and business associates for recommendations. They may have had positive experiences with trust fund lawyers and can provide valuable insight into their professionalism and expertise.
2. Online Research: Search online for trust fund lawyers near you. Online databases such as Avvo and Martindale offer valuable information on estate and trust fund attorneys, including their qualifications, experience, and client reviews.
3. Evaluate Expertise: Make sure the lawyer you choose specializes in trust and estate matters, as they will have the necessary knowledge and experience to handle complex issues related to trust funds. The lawyer should be familiar with various types of trust funds, such as living trusts, special needs trusts, spendthrift trusts, and Medicaid asset protection trusts, to name a few.
4. Assess Communication and Rapport: The trust fund lawyer should communicate well and clearly, answering your questions and addressing your concerns. You should feel comfortable discussing personal matters and have a good rapport, as you will work closely with them throughout the process.
5. Consider Location: Choosing a lawyer with an office near you is helpful. This will make it easier for you to meet with them and attend any necessary appointments.

6. Read Client Reviews: Look for trust fund attorneys with good client reviews. This can provide insight into their expertise, professionalism, and service quality.
7. Determine Motivation and Enthusiasm: A reasonable trust fund attorney should be genuinely interested in helping you achieve your estate planning goals. They should be eager to answer your questions and address your concerns.
8. Consult Multiple Lawyers: Speak with multiple attorneys to find the one that best fits your estate planning and trust fund needs. Discuss your goals and concerns with each attorney and evaluate their expertise and experience.

Critical duties of an estate planning lawyer

Estate planning is integral to asset management, allowing one to control how one's wealth will be distributed upon death. Lawyers specializing in this area guide individuals throughout this process, assisting them in making well-considered decisions and preparing legally binding documents.

Crucial tasks that an estate planning lawyer can undertake:

1. Drafting a Will: The cornerstone of any estate plan, a will, allows the individual to dictate how their assets will be distributed upon their death.

2. Identifying Beneficiaries: A lawyer can help identify and name beneficiaries for various assets, such as life insurance policies, retirement accounts, and other financial holdings. This step ensures the individual's intentions and disbursement of assets.

3. Establishing a Durable Power of Attorney: This legal instrument enables an individual to designate a reliable person to make financial and medical decisions if they become incapacitated. An estate planning lawyer can assist in creating and implementing these documents, ensuring they comply with state laws and are legally binding.

4. Minimizing Estate Taxes: Estate taxes can notably diminish the value of a person's assets. An estate planning attorney can pinpoint strategies to reduce or avoid these taxes, thereby enhancing the wealth inherited by beneficiaries.

5. Bypassing Probate Court: Probate is a legal procedure that settles a deceased person's estate and distributes their assets. It can be lengthy and costly. To bypass this process, an estate planning attorney can suggest strategies such as establishing a revocable living trust or advocating joint ownership of assets.

6. Establishing Trusts: Trusts can protect assets during a person's life and posthumously. An estate planning attorney can assist in setting up suitable trusts to protect assets and ensure they are managed and distributed as per the person's desires.

Hiring the right estate planning attorney more than pays for itself, as the attorney can create a customized estate plan tailored to your specific needs, provide valuable legal advice, and ensure that all decisions are made in accordance with the law. Moreover, having a dedicated professional to consult with regarding questions or concerns and make necessary updates to estate planning documents can offer invaluable peace of mind.

Estate planning attorneys generally charge a flat fee for creating legal documents and/or an hourly rate for ongoing consultation and maintenance of an estate.

"Know thyself" before you call the attorney.

1. Your marital status, the number of children you have, and any other individuals you want to include in your will are all crucial information. Providing this information will help your lawyer understand how to distribute your assets according to your wishes and state laws.

What do your finances look like?

2. Your lawyer will need a comprehensive list of your assets and liabilities to make informed decisions about your financial future. This includes bank accounts, properties, outstanding debts, and other financial obligations.

What is your budget?

3. Attorneys may charge flat fees or hourly rates, depending on the services required. Discussing your budget upfront will help your lawyer develop a compensation model that meets your needs and avoids surprises.

What do you want to give away?

4. After accounting for spousal shares and settling any liabilities, you may have personal bequests you'd like to make. This could include monetary gifts to relatives, trust funds for children, or specific items like heirlooms. Your lawyer will help you incorporate these bequests into your estate plan.

5. While estate planning is typically not time-sensitive, you may want to coordinate with other professionals, such as accountants and financial planners. Ensure you allow enough time to understand your estate plan and its long-term implications comprehensively.

What documents do you have?

6. Reviewing all existing documents and forms with your lawyer is essential to avoid miscommunications and ensure your wishes are clearly expressed in your estate plan.

DIVORCE ISSUES AND ESTATE PLANNING

Divorce issues and estate planning will require some changes to your estate planning paperwork:

- Revocation of beneficiary designations: In many cases, divorce will automatically revoke any beneficiary designations made in favor of the ex-spouse, such as those for life insurance policies, etc. This means that if no new beneficiary is designated, these assets may pass to someone else or be subject to the terms of the will.
- Changes to property ownership: Divorce may result in a change of ownership or title for jointly owned property, which can affect how it is distributed after death. In some cases, updating deeds or other legal documents to reflect these changes may be necessary.
- Disinheriting the ex-spouse: Unless otherwise specified in a prenuptial or postnuptial agreement, divorce may automatically

revoke any gifts or bequests made to favor the ex-spouse in a will or trust. This means the ex-spouse would not be entitled to any inheritance under these documents.

- Changes to the fiduciary roles: In some cases, a spouse may have been appointed as a trustee, executor, or agent under a power of attorney in an estate plan. After a divorce, it may be necessary to update these documents to reflect a new choice of fiduciary.

FAMILY CONFLICTS

Family conflicts over a will or trust fund distribution can be emotionally challenging and legally complex. Here are some steps you can take to help handle these conflicts:

Communicate openly and clearly: One of the best ways to prevent or resolve family conflicts is to communicate clearly and openly with all interested parties. Ensure that everyone understands the terms of the will or trust fund and any relevant legal requirements. Be willing to listen to concerns and respond to questions or feedback.

Consider mediation: If communication has broken down or there are complex legal or emotional issues at play, mediation may be a helpful option. A neutral third-party mediator can help facilitate discussions and work toward a mutually acceptable solution.

Consider the emotional impact: Family conflicts over a will or trust fund can be emotionally charged, particularly if long-standing family dynamics are at play. It's essential to consider the emotional impact on all parties and work towards a fair and respectful resolution.

Follow legal requirements: Following all legal requirements for distributing a will or trust fund is essential. This may include filing the necessary paperwork, obtaining legal advice, and working with a qualified trustee or executor.

Plan ahead: In some cases, conflicts can be avoided by planning and communicating clearly with all family members involved.

Ask around for a referral or contact our office (email: *info@oakwoodwealth.com*), and we'll share our process for using one of our team's network of attorneys available nationwide.

Resolving an Estate Sibling Battle

Unfortunately, navigating through the murky waters of inheritance disputes among siblings is a widespread occurrence after a parent's passing. Such conflicts can trigger protracted, costly legal proceedings. Yet, with meticulous planning and consideration, parents and siblings can proactively take measures to avert or reconcile these disputes.

Formulating an Estate Plan: The Parent's Role

A pivotal step for parents is to draft a will, offering explicit directives about how their assets should be divided. This extends to designating which sibling will inherit specific properties or assets, whether a family home, a business, or priceless works of art. If desired, parents could arrange for the family home to be sold, and the resulting funds equally split among the siblings.

Parents pondering the challenging decision to disinherit a child would be wise to broach this subject with the child or include an explanatory note in the will to fend off potential legal challenges. Establishing a trust can also facilitate clear directions for property distribution post-death. An advantage of a revocable trust is its flexibility—it can be adjusted any time before the parent's passing, given they are mentally competent.

Another proactive stepparent(s) can take is to attach a child's name to assets. This ensures that these assets seamlessly transition to the designated child upon the parent's demise. Appointing a non-sibling executor or trustee can also contribute to a harmonious atmosphere among siblings, as the chosen individual doesn't have a personal stake in the decisions regarding property allocations.

Allocation of Less Significant Items

Parents can also pre-empt conflicts over smaller, sentimental items by giving them as gifts during their lifetime. This strategy makes sure that the value of these items falls below the annual gift tax exclusion, currently $18,000 for the year 2024.

Alternatives include labeling items with the recipient's name or penning a letter of instruction detailing the division of belongings. Although not legally binding, these practices can unmistakably convey the parent's wishes.

Post-Mortem Measures for Siblings

If a parent falls short and doesn't have the foresight to prevent conflicts, siblings can collaborate to uphold harmony and limit disputes. Here are some methods they might consider:

Employing a mediator: For grave disputes, such as those surrounding a family business, an impartial, professional mediator can guide siblings to common ground.

Liquidating assets: When siblings find themselves at an impasse regarding the distribution of certain assets, they can sell them and share the resulting funds.

Deferring to an independent fiduciary: Siblings can forfeit their appointment as executor or trustee, empowering a neutral third party to make calls on asset distribution.

Splitting Up Household Belongings

When it's time to divide everyday household items, siblings can adopt tactics to ensure fairness. These could involve rotating turns to choose items or setting up a random draw where each sibling picks a paper detailing an item. Maintaining open communication and respecting each other's feelings makes navigating this challenging process fairly and peaceably possible.

WHAT TO DO AFTER THE PAPERWORK?

Although finalizing your estate plan paperwork may give a sense of accomplishment, it's crucial to realize that further steps are necessary to cement your plan's effectiveness.

Share your health care directives: Essential elements of an estate plan are your health care documents, which may include a Health Care Proxy and a Living Will. Make sure that these documents are in the hands of your healthcare proxies, primary care doctor, and other medical professionals involved in your care. This enables the assigned individuals to make health-related decisions on your behalf when you can't.

Consider the situation of a couple, let's call them Tom and Mary Brown, who have finalized their estate plan and appointed their grown children as their healthcare agents. They must distribute copies of their health care paperwork to their children and primary care doctors to ensure their wishes are understood and honored.

Re-evaluate beneficiary assignments: Review and revise the beneficiary assignments on assets like life insurance policies, retirement accounts, and annuities to ensure they align with your comprehensive estate plan. Assets with named beneficiaries bypass the probate process and go directly to the designated beneficiaries upon your death. Regular reviews and updates of these assignments are essential to prevent distributions that don't align with your wishes.

Imagine, for example, that Mary Brown had designated her ex-husband as the beneficiary of her life insurance policy before her recent marriage. She should adjust the beneficiary to her current husband or other intended beneficiaries.

Ensure your Trust is funded: If you have a Revocable Living Trust in your estate plan, ensuring your assets are re-titled in the trust's name is critical. This is a crucial step in achieving the trust's objectives, such as avoiding probate and reducing estate tax. Seek assistance from your estate planning professional to retitle your assets accordingly.

For instance, if Tom and Mary Brown have created a Revocable Living Trust, they need to ensure that their assets, encompassing real estate, bank accounts, and investment accounts, are re-titled in the name of the trust.

Deal with property matters: If you're transferring real estate into a trust or different ownership structure, it's wise to engage a lawyer authorized to practice in the state where the property is situated. This ensures that the property transfer complies with local laws and doesn't inadvertently affect property tax exemptions, property insurance coverage, or title insurance coverage. Moreover, moving out-of-state property into a trust can circumvent the need for out-of-state probate proceedings.

For example, Tom and Mary Brown own a holiday home in Florida. They need to engage a Florida-licensed attorney to help transfer the property into their trust.

Keep your plan current: Life changes, whether marriages, divorces, births, deaths, or shifts in financial circumstances, necessitate the regular review and update of your estate plan. Additionally, changes in tax laws over time could affect your estate plan. Regularly revisiting and tweaking your plan ensures it remains aligned with your intentions and delivers the best possible results for you and your loved ones.

Estate Planning Mistakes to Avoid

Estate planning is a complex process, and mistakes can have far-reaching consequences for those persons or entities you make a part of your estate plan. As you develop or update your estate plan, you must be aware of some common errors and avoid them. This guide provides an in-depth discussion of these mistakes and how to prevent them, helping you create a compelling and comprehensive estate plan.

1. Not understanding your matrimonial property regime: Your marriage contract forms the financial basis of your union and provides the framework for your estate plan.

Example: If Tom and Jane are married in a community of property, Tom needs to ensure that his will only deals with his half-share of the joint estate. If they are married with the accrual system, Tom must consider any potential accrual claims that may arise in the event of his death.

2. Providing incorrectly for your minor children:

Example: Susan wants to leave her savings to her children, aged 10 and 14. Instead of bequeathing the money directly, she establishes a testamentary trust that will manage the funds until the children reach the age of majority.

3. Dealing with insurance policies and retirement funds in your will: Life insurance policy proceeds and retirement benefits fall outside of your deceased estate. To avoid confusion, do not mention these assets in your will.

Example: John has a life insurance policy with his wife, Mary, as the beneficiary. He should not include the policy in his will, as the proceeds will be paid directly to Mary upon his death.

4. Getting a beneficiary to witness your will: Beneficiaries who also sign as witnesses can be disqualified from inheriting. Ensure that those who stand to benefit from your will do not act as witnesses.

Example: If Jane's daughter is a beneficiary in her will, she should not also serve as a witness to avoid potential disqualification from inheriting.

5. Not updating your will after your divorce: Update your will as soon as your divorce order is granted. Failure to do so can result in your ex-spouse inadvertently inheriting from your estate.

Example: After his divorce from Karen, Tom should revise his will to remove her as a beneficiary and avoid the risk of her inheriting his assets.

6. Not dating your will: Although not a requirement for validity, dating your will helps ensure that there is no confusion about which version is the most recent.

Example: Sarah has drafted several versions of her will over the years. By dating each one, she clarifies which document represents her latest wishes.

7. Getting your beneficiary nomination wrong: Ensure you nominate the correct beneficiaries in your life policies, especially if you intend to use them to create liquidity in your estate.

Example: If Frank wants the proceeds of his life insurance policy to cover his estate's liabilities and costs, he should nominate his estate as the beneficiary.

8. Nominating a minor child as a beneficiary to a life policy after divorce: Consider the consequences of naming your minor child as a beneficiary, as they cannot inherit, and your ex-spouse may end up managing the funds.

Example: After divorcing her husband, Lisa named their 12-year-old son as the beneficiary of her life insurance policy.

CHAPTER SUMMARY

Estate planning is essential in safeguarding your financial future, providing for your family and loved ones, and leaving a lasting impact. While multiple tactics can be employed in estate planning, your unique goals and circumstances will determine the most effective one. Below, you'll find some of the most widely used estate planning techniques and examples to aid in discerning the strategy most compatible with your requirements.

Forming a Will:

A will is typically the cornerstone of any estate plan. This legal document details the distribution of your assets following your death. By clearly specifying your wishes, you can mitigate possible conflicts among family members and ensure that your estate is partitioned in accordance with your desires.

Consider a woman named Lisa, who has two grown-up children and four grandchildren. In her will, she makes specific bequests, such as assigning her vacation home to her daughter, her investment assets to her son, and setting up educational trust funds for her grandchildren.

Setting up Trusts:

Let's take the scenario of a woman named Bella, who has a special needs son. Bella sets up a special needs trust to ensure her son has the necessary financial resources throughout his life, without endangering his eligibility for public assistance programs.

Appointing Beneficiaries:

Consider the case of a woman named Linda who owns a sizable 401(k) account and a life insurance policy. Linda nominates her two adult children as primary beneficiaries, and her grandchildren as secondary beneficiaries to ensure these assets go directly to her children upon her death.

Powers of Attorney and Health Care Directives:

Estate planning isn't only about posthumous distribution of your assets; it also encompasses planning for possible incapacity.

For instance, a woman named Emma has been diagnosed with an illness that may render her incapacitated in the future. Emma can establish a durable power of attorney for finances, naming her daughter to oversee her financial matters, and a health care directive, appointing her son to make healthcare decisions on her behalf.

Charitable Contributions:

Incorporating philanthropy into your estate plan can not only uphold the causes close to your heart but also offer tax advantages for your estate.

For example, suppose you're committed to supporting research for heart disease. You can include a bequest in your will, bequeathing a part of your estate to a heart research foundation and also name the same organization as a beneficiary of your life insurance policy.

CHAPTER THREE

OLD AGE & INCAPACITY

Let our advance worrying become advanced thinking and planning.

- Winston Churchill

DEMENTIA AND PLANNING AHEAD

As we age, there's a potential for diminishing cognitive abilities, development of paranoia or delusions, or even a complete loss of self-recognition. If you are diagnosed with brain shrinkage, dementia, or a similar condition, it's crucial to make decisions with your family at the earliest opportunity. This prepares you and your loved ones for possible future complications and ensures your preferences are honored in the long run.

Dementia, Anticipatory Decisions, and Anticipatory Statements

When diagnosed with dementia, it may be prudent to write an anticipatory decision or anticipatory statement. These documents permit you to dictate your care and treatment for a time when you may no longer be able to make those decisions independently.

Anticipatory Decisions

An anticipatory decision allows you to decline certain medical treatments under specific conditions and only becomes effective when you no longer possess the mental capacity to make that decision. If done correctly, your anticipatory decision is legally binding, and healthcare providers are obligated to respect it.

Anticipatory Statements

Conversely, an anticipatory statement is an expression of your future preferences. It can cover a wider array of subjects than an anticipatory decision, encompassing refusals and requests for certain types of treatment and care. Although it's not legally binding, it provides insight into your personal values and beliefs and should be considered when others are making decisions on your behalf.

Establishing a Durable Power of Attorney

Even if you haven't made an anticipatory decision or anticipatory statement, you can still set up a durable power of attorney (DPA) for health and welfare. This allows the person(s) you appoint as your attorney(s) to make decisions about your care and treatment, always acting in your best interests. It's important to have frank discussions with your attorney(s) about your preferences so they can make decisions on your behalf with as much confidence as possible.

Involvement of Professionals in Decision-Making

In the absence of a DPA, professionals like physicians and caregiving staff can make decisions for you. They are required to consider your past and current wishes, feelings, beliefs, and values, and seek input from those close to you about these. If possible, they should support you in making the decision yourself and only make decisions for you if you can't.

LEGAL DOCUMENTS FOR PLANNING STAGES

Living Will and advanced directives

The creation of advance directives involves a written document that fulfills your state's legal conditions. While you might consider hiring a lawyer, it's usually not required. After completion, store the original documents in a secure yet reachable location, provide copies to your doctor and healthcare agent, and inform your family about your directives. You should also carry a card in your wallet that mentions you have advance directives and indicates where a copy is available.

Regularly reviewing and updating your advance directives is crucial, especially following significant life events or changes in your health condition. Ensure your updated directives replace previous versions in your medical records and inform your healthcare agent and family of any modifications.

In certain states, an extra document known as Physician Orders for Life-Sustaining Treatment (POLST) can be used by people with severe illnesses. Completed by your doctor, this document serves as a directive to ensure you receive the treatments you prefer in an emergency. The POLST should be placed prominently where healthcare professionals can quickly locate it.

HCP: Health Care Proxy

There are times when unexpected events can render us unable to make important decisions, especially when it concerns our health care. This might occur because of an accident, illness, or a sudden debilitating condition. In such instances, having a dependable person to take charge and make critical decisions on our behalf becomes extremely important. This person is often referred to as a healthcare agent, someone we trust, like a close friend or family member, who is authorized to make healthcare decisions for us when we cannot do so ourselves. While this principle is broadly applicable, specific laws governing the appointment of such a person vary by region.

You may grant your health care agent as much or as little authority as you wish, and even provide instructions they must adhere to. This form can also be used to document your preferences regarding organ, eye, and tissue donation.

When appointing a healthcare agent, it's essential to choose someone you trust and who is willing to take on the responsibility. Be sure to discuss your healthcare wishes and the details of the Health Care Proxy form with your chosen agent and provide them with a signed copy. If you can make healthcare decisions for yourself, you retain the right to do so, and your agent's decision-making power will only come into effect when your doctor determines you are unable to make those decisions.

However, there are some restrictions regarding naming a doctor or a staff member from a hospital, nursing home, or mental hygiene facility where you are a patient or resident as your agent. Ensure you understand these restrictions before appointing a healthcare agent.

Engaging in clear and straightforward conversations about your healthcare preferences with your designated representative is crucial. These talks should include your feelings about different treatment options under various circumstances, enabling your representative to make decisions that align with your wishes and best interests.

Designating a healthcare representative is a smart move even if you are young and in excellent health. This individual will be authorized to act on your behalf should a situation arise where you're temporarily unable to make your own healthcare decisions, such as when under general anesthesia or recovering from an accident. Once you can make decisions again, the authority bestowed upon your representative will be revoked.

It's important to remember that you retain the flexibility to change your mind. Cancelling your health care proxy, replacing your representative, or modifying any stipulations on the form is a straightforward process. Simply complete a new form. Unless an expiry date is indicated or specific events are detailed to nullify it, the health care proxy remains active indefinitely.

Your healthcare representative cannot be held legally responsible for decisions made in good faith on your behalf. This crucial role empowers your chosen representative to advocate for your healthcare preferences when you're unable to do so. By assigning a healthcare representative, you exercise control over your medical treatment, assuring that your desires will be respected, even when you can't express them yourself.

POA: Power of Attorney

The scope of the agent's duties can be wide-ranging, covering decisions about the principal's property, finances, investments, or healthcare. The extent of the agent's authority can be broad or specific, depending on the details of the POA document.

There are primarily two kinds of POAs: financial and healthcare. Each kind gives the attorney-in-fact either general or restricted powers, based on the requirements and wishes of the principal.

A financial POA grants the agent the ability to manage the principal's financial affairs and property issues. The duties of the agent could encompass managing bank accounts, signing checks, selling assets, overseeing properties, and filing taxes on behalf of the principal.

On the other hand, a healthcare POA, often termed a healthcare proxy, permits the agent to make medical decisions on the principal's behalf during a health crisis or if the principal becomes incapacitated. This specific kind of POA is only activated when the principal is no longer able to make healthcare decisions independently.

Key Factors in Establishing a Power of Attorney

When establishing a POA, it's vital to choose a trusted individual who can competently handle the responsibilities outlined in the agreement. This person can be a family member, a close friend, or a reputable professional with expertise in the relevant area.

To set up a POA, you can utilize a template specific to your state or consult an attorney specializing in family law. The principal's signature must be notarized, and in some states, witnesses' signatures may also require notarization.

Power of Attorney Termination and Considerations

A POA can end under various circumstances, such as the principal's death or revocation of the agreement, a court's invalidation, or the agent's inability to fulfill their duties. In the case of a married couple, a divorce may also render the POA invalid.

Anyone planning for potential incapacitation or long-term care should consider establishing a POA. This legal instrument can also be helpful for individuals who expect to be away from home and difficult to reach for an extended period.

Choosing a Power of Attorney: Trustworthiness and Capability

The selection of an agent is a critical decision, as this individual will wield significant authority and responsibility over the principal's affairs. The chosen agent should be trustworthy, capable, and able to act in the principal's best interests.

Parents often designate their adult children as agents under a POA. In such cases, the principal should carefully evaluate each child's trustworthiness, abilities, and capacity to act on their behalf. It's possible to create multiple POAs with different agents, tailoring each POA to the specific skills and capabilities of each child.

Potential Risks and Safeguards

The agent's actions can have far-reaching consequences, so it's essential to ensure they will follow the principal's instructions and act in their best interests. To minimize risks, the POA can require the agent to periodically report their actions to an external party, such as a family attorney or accountant.

As circumstances change, it's crucial to review and update the POA documents. A POA can be revoked by writing a notarized letter that identifies the agreement and states the intention to revoke it. A new POA can then be created and delivered to the newly chosen agent.

DNRO: Do Not Resuscitate Order

A do-not-resuscitate order (DNR) is a legal directive authorized by a medical practitioner at the request of a patient. It signifies that medical staff should not attempt to revive the patient if they experience cardiac arrest or stop breathing. This decision can be challenging and calls for the patient, provided they are competent, and their family, with the patient's consent, to partake in the decision-making process.

Resuscitation might involve various procedures, such as chest compressions, intubation, cardioversion, and IV medication administration. However, it's crucial to understand that resuscitation can be complex and entail significant risks and complications. For instance, chest compressions could result in fractured ribs, punctured lungs, or even heart damage. Furthermore, individuals who are resuscitated might experience brain damage due to decreased blood flow to the brain and subsequent irregular cell activity when blood flow resumes.

Survival rates following resuscitation can differ significantly depending on factors like the patient's age, overall health, and the location of the cardiac arrest (within a hospital or outside). For some patients, particularly those with terminal illnesses or poor prognoses, the risks associated with resuscitation may overshadow the potential benefits. In such instances, a DNR order could be contemplated to assure a more natural and dignified passing.

DNR orders can go by different names, such as "no code" or "allow natural death" (AND) orders. A physician must write and sign these orders, including the patient's name and date. The rules and regulations concerning DNR orders can differ from one state to another, making it critical to familiarize oneself with the specific requirements in the patient's locale.

To ensure a DNR order is upheld, patients should keep a hard copy of the order easily accessible and notify paramedics or other medical professionals of its existence when necessary. Traveling with a copy of the DNR order and wearing a medical ID indicating the patient's DNR status can also be useful.

While a DNR order provides clear guidance to healthcare providers not to resuscitate, it's essential to remember that a DNR does not address other aspects of medical care such as pain management or nutrition. Inconsistencies in the application of DNR orders can sometimes lead to less-than-optimal care for patients with a DNR in place.

The consideration of a DNR order can be emotionally fraught, necessitating open and sincere discussions with your healthcare provider and your family about your desires and the potential ramifications. Evaluating the benefits and risks of resuscitation in the context of your health or a loved one's health is a crucial step in making an informed decision.

WHY WOULD YOU NEED TO CREATE A TRUST

When faced with the reality of a family member diagnosed with dementia, it is crucial to ensure their financial affairs and care are properly managed. Creating a trust allows you to appoint family members or trusted professionals as trustees to continue overseeing the finances and well-being of the affected individual.

Understanding Revocable and Irrevocable Trusts

This type of trust provides for successor trustees, who can manage your assets and care if you become disabled or face age-related challenges, such as dementia. The transfer of control over your assets and care happens outside the court process, making it more efficient and less costly.

While a revocable living trust does not typically reduce estate tax obligations, it can help avoid probate. This type of trust enables a trustee to manage the property according to your direction if you become incapacitated, and upon your death, distribute the property to beneficiaries or continue managing the trust in their interest.

An irrevocable trust, on the other hand, cannot be modified, changed, or revoked once it becomes effective. This type of trust provides greater protection of assets from creditors and can be utilized for avoiding federal estate taxes on estates larger than the current exemption amount.

Estate Planning for Dementia and Assisted Living Scenarios

Dementia, which is not considered a normal part of aging, can impact various cognitive functions such as attention span, language skills, visual perception, and self-management. Considering the prevalence of dementia among older adults, it is essential to engage in proper estate planning to protect your estate, family, and personal care.

It is vital to act promptly when it comes to estate planning for individuals with dementia. Once a person is no longer able to understand their assets or the purpose of estate planning documents, it may be too late for them to participate in the process. Key considerations in helping a person with dementia plan for the future include health care and long-term care, financial planning, and appointing another person to make decisions on their behalf.

Benefits of a Revocable Living Trust

It is the ideal vehicle for planning your future care and establishing pathways for successors and beneficiaries to fulfill your wishes. Advantages of using a revocable living trust include:

- Allowing successor trustees to manage your assets
- Stating your care preferences (home care, assisted living, etc.)
- Naming multiple backup options for your successor trustee
- Offering flexibility in terms and conditions for your care based on your preferences.

Establishing a revocable living trust ensures that your care preferences are followed, protecting you and your partner during your lifetimes, and enabling a seamless transfer of assets. This estate planning strategy helps avoid the costs and delays associated with probate and conservatorships.

COURT-APPOINTED Guardians and administrators

As we explore the topic of court-appointed guardians and administrators, it is crucial to understand the role these individuals play in the lives of those who are unable to care for themselves. This is especially relevant when the person in question is suffering from dementia, as their cognitive abilities may be significantly impaired. In such cases, a supportive guardian or administrator can be of immense help, ensuring that the individual's caregiving, financial, and legal matters are taken care of properly. Most often, this responsibility is entrusted to a close relative, but the court must authorize the appointment.

Recent media reports have brought attention to the increasing prevalence of guardianships, with instances such as that of pop star Britney Spears coming to the fore. Guardianships, also known as conservatorships, are designed to safeguard individuals unable to handle their financial or health-related matters due to mental incapacitation, which can occur due to Alzheimer's disease or other types of dementia.

Physical support options are often needed for both the carer and the dementia patient. These services can significantly improve the quality of life for those affected by dementia and can provide valuable respite for their caregivers. It is always beneficial to explore the various support options available, as some may be provided free or subsidized by your medical care plan. Such options can include:

- Home visits from caregivers
- Modifications to the household
- Community centers for daytime activities
- Temporary relief care, also known as 'substitute care'
- Assistance from experts, such as a nurse specializing in dementia
- Community support circles
- Psychotherapy sessions
- Customized information to fulfill your specific requirements

Home care serves as a critical aid for numerous dementia patients, facilitating their ability to remain in their own familiar surroundings while benefiting from necessary assistance and care. This service also provides substantial relief and support to caregivers. Home care services encompass an extensive array of aids, from nonmedical support with daily life activities to professional health services administered by licensed healthcare experts such as nurses or physiotherapists.

Different forms of home care services include:

- Friendly companionship - offering company, overseeing safety, recreational activities, or social calls.
- Personal hygiene assistance.
- Home maintenance services.
- Professional healthcare.

To find suitable home care services, you should tap into several resources:

- Consult with the patient's primary doctor for recommendations of home healthcare providers proficient in dementia care.
- Alzheimer's Association – www.alz.org
- National Association of Social Workers – www.socialworkers.org
- U.S. Dept of Health and Human Services – www.Alzheimers.gov
- Local Senior Care facilities often have additional insight.

WHO WILL DO MOST OF THE CARING?

Caring for a loved one with dementia is a challenging and emotional journey, and it often raises the question: who will be responsible for providing most of the care? This issue can quickly become a hot topic within families and requires sensitive handling to ensure that all parties feel supported and heard. When addressing the matter of caregiving responsibilities, there are several key considerations to keep in mind:

The main carer has the right to request extra support and assistance: It is essential to recognize that the primary caregiver may require additional help on various levels, including emotional, physical, and financial support. Family members and friends should be prepared to offer their assistance when needed and be open to discussing the primary caregiver's needs and concerns.

Sharing care responsibilities more equally: Ideally, caregiving duties should be distributed among family members and friends to prevent the primary caregiver from becoming overwhelmed. This can be achieved by delegating specific tasks or arranging a rotating schedule to ensure that everyone contributes to the care of a loved one. It is crucial to consider each person's strengths, availability, and comfort level when determining how to divide the responsibilities.

Establishing good communication: Open and honest communication is vital in caregiving. All parties involved should feel comfortable discussing their feelings, concerns, and needs related to the care of the loved one. Regular family meetings or check-ins can be an excellent way to maintain communication and address any issues that arise.

Demonstrating empathy: Caring for a loved one with dementia can be an emotional and exhausting experience. It is crucial for all family members and friends involved in the care process to demonstrate empathy and understanding for one another's feelings and experiences. This support can help to create a positive environment for the loved one and those providing care.

Focusing on the main goal: Ultimately, the primary objective of caregiving is to ensure that the loved one with dementia is well cared for and as happy and healthy as possible. All parties involved should prioritize this goal and work collaboratively to create a care plan that meets the individual's needs and preferences. It is essential to find ways to work together as a team to ensure the best possible care and support for your loved one. Here are six tips to help families collaborate effectively in dementia care:

1. Communicate Regularly: The behavioral symptoms of dementia can change frequently, making regular communication among family members crucial. If you are the primary caregiver, keep everyone informed of your loved one's condition and any challenges you are facing. Stay connected through phone calls, emails, letters, or social media to ensure that everyone is on the same page.

2. Empathize: Everyone reacts differently to difficult situations, so try to understand your family members' perspectives before getting upset or angry. This empathetic approach can help you find solutions that prioritize the well-being of your loved one with dementia. For example, if a sibling is emotionally unable to cope with the situation, they may be able to contribute in other ways, such as providing financial support.

3. Ask for Help: If you feel overwhelmed by caregiving responsibilities, let your family know without complaining or blaming others. They may not realize how much you are struggling unless you share your challenges and ask for specific support. Remember that many hands make light work, and sharing the caregiving burden can alleviate stress and improve the well-being of all involved.

4. Make Decisions Together: Even if you are the primary caregiver, involve your family in major care decisions. Discuss the pros, cons, and financial considerations of various options before deciding. Including everyone's thoughts and opinions can help avoid resentment and ensure that everyone feels heard and valued.

5. Leave Childhood Rivalries Behind: It can be challenging but try to approach caregiving as an adult, not as the younger person your siblings or family members may still perceive you as. Family conflicts often stem from unresolved issues from childhood or disagreements over a loved one's capabilities, financial matters, or caregiving responsibilities. Recognizing how past issues influence your current relationships can provide a fresh perspective and help you navigate present challenges more effectively.

6. Enlist the Help of a Mediator: When family conflicts become too complex or emotionally charged, consider seeking the assistance of a third-party professional, such as a counselor, mediator, or geriatric care manager. An impartial voice of reason can help guidc your family toward resolution and collaboration.

HOW DO YOU DECIDE WHEN TO GET EXTRA HELP

Deciding when to seek additional help or consider placing your loved one in a memory care facility is an important and challenging decision. Several factors come into play, and ultimately, the decision will depend on the unique circumstances of your loved one and your family. Here are some key considerations to help you make the best decision for your loved one:

Assess the current care situation: Begin by evaluating the present caregiving arrangements. Consider whether the current care is meeting the needs of your loved one and if the caregiving responsibilities are becoming too overwhelming for you or other family members. Keep in mind that dementia is a progressive condition, and the required level of care may change over time.

Monitor your loved one's health and safety: Observe your loved one's health, safety, and overall well-being. Signs that your loved one may need additional help or specialized care include increased confusion, disorientation, or wandering; frequent falls or accidents; weight loss or poor hygiene; and unmanageable behavioral issues such as aggression or agitation.

Evaluate the level of assistance required: Determine the type and amount of assistance your loved one needs, including help with daily living activities, medication management, mobility, and supervision. If these needs exceed what you or other caregivers can reasonably provide at home, it may be time to consider additional support or a memory care facility.

Assess the impact on the primary caregiver's health and well-being: Caregiving can take a significant toll on the physical and emotional health of the primary caregiver. It is crucial to consider the caregiver's well-being and whether the current caregiving situation is sustainable in the long term. If the caregiver's health is suffering or their quality of life is being negatively affected, it may be time to seek extra help or explore memory care options.

Consider the financial implications: Memory care facilities can be costly, so it is essential to review your family's financial resources and evaluate the affordability of various care options.

Explore memory care facility options: Research different memory care facilities in your area and take the time to visit each one. Consider factors such as staff training and expertise, the facility's environment and amenities, the care services provided, and the staff-to-resident ratio. Speak with other families who have placed their loved ones in memory care facilities to gain insight into their experiences.

Seek professional guidance: Consult with medical professionals, such as your loved one's physician, a geriatric care manager, or a social worker, to discuss the best course of action. These professionals can provide valuable insights and recommendations based on their expertise and familiarity with your loved one's specific needs.

Engage in open communication with family members: Keep an open dialogue with your family members throughout the decision-making process. Consider everyone's opinions and concerns and aim to reach a consensus on what is best for your loved one.

Recognizing when it is time for a loved one with dementia to receive additional help or be placed in a memory care facility can be a challenging decision. Dementia symptoms may vary day-to-day or even moment-to-moment, making it difficult to determine when a change in living arrangements or care level is necessary. Nonetheless, it is important to discuss concerns early on and consult with medical professionals to ensure the safety and well-being of your loved one.

Doctors evaluating patients for dementia will typically focus on their ability to perform daily tasks, known as activities of daily living (ADLs), and their overall safety. Some red flags that may indicate a need for memory care include disorientation, agitation, difficulty in conversation, or noticeable changes in appearance, such as disheveled hair or weight loss. Furthermore, doctors may assess the patient's ability to complete daily tasks such as dressing, bathing, and using the restroom. Struggles in these areas may suggest that 24-hour care is necessary.

Safety concerns are another crucial factor in determining the need for memory care. Doctors may inquire about any incidents that could indicate a lack of safety, such as leaving appliances on, failing to care for pets, unexplained injuries, or wandering into dangerous situations. It is essential to consider whether the individual's safety needs are being met and whether additional support would improve their well-being.

In addition to assessing daily functioning and safety, doctors may conduct mental status exams to determine the level of cognitive decline. These brief assessments can help track changes in memory, concentration, and spatial awareness, providing valuable information for determining the most appropriate care.

When evaluating whether memory care is the right option, consider asking yourself the following questions:

1. Have friends or family members noticed changes in behavior?
2. Does your loved one exhibit agitation or aggression?
3. Is your aging relative withdrawn or nervous?
4. Are their hygiene needs met?
5. Does your loved one wander?
6. Are their living conditions safe?
7. Are their medications properly managed?
8. Is your loved one well-nourished?
9. Have you started to feel caregiver burnout?
10. Is caring for your loved one going well?
11. Are you feeling resentful towards them?
12. Is caregiving affecting your health?
13. Are you and your family safe?

These questions can help you assess your family's situation and determine whether memory care is an appropriate choice. In cases where dementia behaviors become unmanageable, seeking guidance from professionals, and exploring memory care facilities can provide the necessary support to ensure your loved one's safety and well-being.

ACTION CHECKLIST

Here is a to-do checklist based on the main points of the chapter:

To-Do Checklist:

☐ Prepare Legal Documents.

☐ Advance Directive: Document detailing your preferences for medical care.

☐ Medical Power of Attorney.

☐ Durable Power of Attorney. Assign an individual to manage your financial and legal matters if you become incapacitated.

☐ Do Not Resuscitate Order. Your wishes for resuscitation measures.

☐ Create a Trust. To ensure your assets are managed according to your wishes.

☐ Plan for Extra Medical Care Needs.

☐ Address potential dementia or conditions requiring additional support.

☐ Determine who will provide care - family members, in-home nurses, assisted living, etc.

☐ Decide when you will need to bring in additional help.

☐ As health conditions progress and daily tasks become challenging.

☐ If living alone when safety and wellbeing become a concern.

☐ When family members need respite from providing full-time care.

☐ Court-Appointed Guardians: Only needed if no advance directives are in place and the person is deemed incapacitated.

☐ Review and Revise: Review all preparations with family and legal/medical professionals. Make any needed changes as health or living situations change.

☐ Inform and Educate: Make all your wishes known to family and friends to avoid confusion or disagreements about your care. Provide copies of legal documents.

It is natural to ponder what might happen to our loved ones if something were to happen to us. This question becomes more pressing as we age and approach retirement, and it is crucial to address these concerns head-on to achieve peace of mind.

As you move through this book, you'll discover strategies and tools designed to help you plan for and protect your loved ones' well-being in the event of your passing or incapacitation. By taking a proactive approach to estate planning, you can ensure that your family is cared for according to your wishes, and that your hard-earned wealth is preserved and distributed as you intended.

First, it is essential to consider the financial aspects of your estate plan. Establishing a will or trust can help you outline your wishes for asset distribution and minimize potential conflicts among your family members. By doing so, you can alleviate the burden on your loved ones during an emotionally challenging time and prevent the erosion of your estate due to taxes, legal fees, or other complications.

Next, it is vital to think about the care of any minor or incapacitated children or grandchildren who may rely on you. With proper estate planning, you can appoint a guardian and establish financial provisions for their well-being, ensuring that they continue to receive the care and support they need even after you are gone.

Through charitable giving or establishing a family foundation, you can support causes that align with your values and create a lasting impact on your community and the world. By doing this, you not only contribute to the greater good but also set an inspiring example for your children, grandchildren, and loved ones to follow.

Finally, while it might seem challenging to tackle these topics, remember that professional help is available to assist you. As you navigate the complex legal and financial landscape, estate planning attorneys, financial advisors, and tax professionals can provide invaluable guidance and support. If you are not sure where to begin, simply call or email us, and our team will assist you or, at minimum, point you in the right direction.

CHAPTER FOUR

PROTECTING & PROVIDING FOR YOUR FAMILY

Family means no one gets left behind or forgotten.

- David Ogden Stiers

WHAT HAPPENS WHEN YOU DIE?

The cycle of life includes the inevitability of death and the associated legal and fiscal procedures that come in its aftermath. When someone dies, their loved ones must wade through intricate tax, financial, and legal processes to settle the decedent's estate. This guide is intended to shed light on some of the obstacles that bereaved relatives may encounter.

Determining if the deceased person left behind a will is the primary step. Should a will exist, it usually identifies an executor responsible for overseeing the asset transfer, satisfying outstanding debts, submitting income tax returns, and distributing any leftover assets as per the will's stipulations. Without a will, the assets will be allocated to the rightful heirs according to state law, and the court will assign an executor.

Nonetheless, there are circumstances when an executor may not be obligatory.

The executor or the nearest kin must secure multiple copies of the death certificate, available at the funeral home. These certificates are indispensable for informing financial institutions, government agencies, insurance companies, and others about the demise.

While the deceased's estate is answerable for debts, the family generally isn't unless the debts were jointly held or co-signed. Still, this could impact the family since any money or assets must first be used to settle the deceased's debts before distribution to the survivors.

If an heir decides to inhabit a property with a mortgage, they must carry on with the mortgage payments. This is tricky as most lenders will want the occupant to qualify for a loan and may accelerate the mortgage to be due immediately. Insurance can be an asset to pay off the mortgage. Planning is crucial here. Alternatively, they could sell the property to settle the existing loan.

In rental property situations, the lease doesn't terminate immediately upon the person's death. The decedent's estate remains liable for rental payments until the lease ends, or a new tenant occupies the premises.

Auto loans and similar debts are under the purview of the executor, who needs to manage these debts using the estate's resources. Creditors have a claim against the decedent's estate, and the executor must clear the deceased's debts with their assets.

Furthermore, the executor has the duty to recover any debts owed to the deceased. Proper documentation of these debts is crucial for the executor to identify and collect them.

Lastly, handling emails and other online accounts is a pertinent question. Different companies have varying rules about managing accounts following the user's death. Hence, it's crucial to familiarize oneself with the policies of each service the deceased uses. Actions may encompass memorializing accounts, deleting accounts and their data, or collaborating with the company to deactivate accounts and remove specific content.

Think through which documents you can organize in advance. For example, have a clear view of how you bank accounts are titled and how they should look in the future.

An effective strategy to ensure your heirs can swiftly access your account posthumously is to assign transfer-on-death (TOD) beneficiaries to your account. By nominating a TOD or POD (Pay On Death) beneficiary, your assets can evade probate, facilitating a less strenuous and more prompt transfer of funds to your designated successors. While your beneficiaries are unable to access your account until after your demise, you retain the right to alter the named beneficiaries at any given moment.

The presence of a will is another pivotal element of estate planning. Despite a will not eliminating the probate process, it can offer directions on how assets are distributed and avert potential disagreements among your heirs. It's worth noting that assets transferred via a will may still be liable to estate taxes, and the probate process could be lengthy and expensive.

Establishing a trust could also prove advantageous as it can sidestep probate and potentially lessen the tax liability for your heirs. However, the creation and maintenance of a trust can be costly, and trusts are not uniform. It's crucial to confirm that your bank accounts are either retitled to the trust or have a designated POD beneficiary.

Adding joint account holders possessing survivorship rights is another method to simplify the asset transfer post-death. This setup permits the surviving account holder(s) to inherit the account by default. Nonetheless, potential drawbacks of this arrangement should be contemplated while you're alive, such as the possibility of gift tax implications and unauthorized withdrawals by co-account holders.

If no preparations are made for your bank account before your demise, the account will likely undergo probate and be allocated according to your state's regulations. An executor would be appointed to oversee your estate, and after settling any outstanding debts, the remaining assets will be dispensed to your spouse, children, or other designated heirs. In instances where there are no surviving relatives or nominated beneficiaries, the estate's funds might be transferred to the state.

WHAT BECOMES OF UNSETTLED DEBTS?

When an individual dies with outstanding debts, it's natural for the surviving spouse or other heirs to question the fate of these liabilities. The handling of these debts depends on the nature of the debt and the relevant state laws.

Usually, creditors try to reclaim what's due by targeting the decedent's estate through a process known as probate. The estate includes the deceased's assets such as financial accounts, personal belongings, and real estate. However, not all assets are deemed part of the estate for probate purposes. Most of the time, the surviving spouse or other beneficiaries are not accountable for the debt, though there can be exceptions.

Probate is the procedure of settling all remaining debts and distributing any leftover assets from the estate to heirs. Each state has its regulations stipulating the duration creditors have to make a claim against the estate during probate. This period can be a few months in some states and up to several years in others. State laws also dictate the precedence of debt payments from the estate. Generally, funeral expenses are prioritized, followed by the estate's administration costs, taxes, and then medical bills.

Certain assets like life insurance policies, eligible retirement accounts, and specific types of trusts avoid probate and directly pass on to the named beneficiary. Jointly owned property, such as a house, can also evade probate if titled correctly. Occasionally, a person may die with an insolvent estate, unable to cover its liabilities, yet still transfer assets that didn't go through probate and are typically untouchable by creditors.

In states practicing "community property" laws, assets and certain debts accrued during marriage are equally owned by both spouses. This implies that a surviving spouse could be liable for the debt repayment, even if it was solely in the decedent's name. However, a well-crafted letter accompanied by a death certificate could result in the debt being dismissed. Through the probate process, you notify the company that the estate possesses minimal or no assets to cover the debt and request its forgiveness.

If you co-own debt, like cosigning a loan, you must continue payments if the other party dies. It's important to note that federal student loans are dismissed if the student passes away. Loans often taken out by parents to cover education expenses not addressed by other financial aids are discharged if the student or the parent who acquired the loan dies.

WHAT HAPPENS IF YOU DIE INTESTATE?

Dying without a will is referred to as dying "intestate." In such cases, state intestacy laws determine how the deceased person's assets are distributed among their heirs.

The Importance of Having a Will

When you pass away without a will, your final wishes remain unknown, leaving the distribution of your estate in the hands of the probate court. This situation, known as dying intestate, can have negative consequences for your loved ones, causing additional stress, financial burden, and potential disputes among family members. Therefore, creating a comprehensive will is essential to ensure that your assets, family, and legacy are handled according to your preferences.

A last will and testament allow you to control various aspects of your estate, such as choosing your heirs, nominating guardians for minor children, assigning caretakers for your pets, and providing instructions for resolving debts and taxes. Additionally, crafting a will enables you to establish your legacy by giving to nonprofit organizations and distributing specific assets or property to designated beneficiaries.

The Probate Process and Its Implications

The probate procedure, which directs the dispersal of your possessions after your demise, can be time-consuming and expensive, particularly for extensive or intricate estates. Additionally, the lack of a will can exacerbate issues as the court must designate a personal representative to oversee your estate. Occasionally, if nobody is prepared or capable of managing your estate, the court may assign a public trustee to regulate the allocation of your assets.

While certain estates might circumvent intestacy proceedings through revocable living trusts, co-owned property, transfer-on-death accounts, or other methods, formulating a will remains a wise decision for anyone, irrespective of their estate's size. By crafting a will, you can ensure the well-being of your loved ones and pets after your death and direct the distribution of your estate according to your explicit wishes.

The Consequences of Dying Intestate

Dying without a will can have several negative effects on your loved ones, such as:

- The court's decisions on matters like the appointment of an executor, the nomination of guardians for minor children, and the handling of debts and taxes may not align with your wishes.
- The distribution of your assets will be determined by local intestate succession laws, which may not reflect your personal preferences.

- The lack of a will can lead to disagreements and conflicts among your family members, potentially resulting in lengthy legal battles.

A well-crafted will is crucial to safeguarding your family's well-being and ensuring that your estate is managed according to your desires.

Creating a Will: Options and Considerations

There are several ways to create a will, ranging from hiring a lawyer to using online self-help services. If your estate is complex or you have specific wishes that need to be addressed, working with a team, (Attorney, CPA, Financial Planner) will be the best option.

How do you make a will without a lawyer?

To make a will without a lawyer, follow these general steps:

1. Research your state's requirements for a valid will, such as the number of witnesses needed and whether it must be notarized.
2. Write a clear and concise statement expressing that this document is your last will and testament and that you revoke any previous wills.
3. Name an executor who will be responsible for administering your estate according to your wishes.
4. Specify your beneficiaries and the assets you wish to leave to each of them.
5. Offer directions for settling debts, taxes, and additional costs associated with your estate.
6. If relevant, designate a guardian for your underage children and offer guidance for their sustenance and support.

7. Authenticate and timestamp the will in the company of the necessary number of witnesses, who should also authenticate and timestamp the document.
8. Store the will in a safe and accessible location and inform your executor of its whereabouts.

For simpler estates, online self-help services can offer a more cost-effective solution. These services typically provide standardized templates that can be customized to your specific situation, allowing you to create a legally valid will with relative ease. Once you have completed your will, be sure to follow the necessary steps to have it signed and witnessed, as required by your state's laws.

Last Wills and Testaments

The importance of creating a will cannot be overstated. It is an essential document that ensures your wishes are fulfilled after your passing and can alleviate confusion or conflict among your loved ones. Even though 70% of Americans don't have a will, the process is relatively simple and can be accomplished without the assistance of a lawyer for many people.

First, you must decide which type will best suit your needs. A simple will, or last will and testament, is sufficient for most individuals. However, if your estate is more complex, you might consider a living trust. Consult an estate attorney if you're uncertain.

Next, determine which assets to include in your will. This list should encompass your property, bank, and retirement accounts, life insurance policies, and pets. It is also important to consider any family heirlooms or personal items of sentimental value that you would like to designate for specific individuals.

Once you have cataloged your assets, it's time to choose your beneficiaries. These are the people who will inherit your assets after your passing. Beneficiaries may include immediate family members, extended family, friends, or even charities you support. Be very specific when designating assets to your beneficiaries to avoid disputes and or confusion in the future.

Now you must choose an executor for your will. This person is responsible for carrying out your final wishes, distributing property to beneficiaries, and addressing any debts you may have. Select someone reliable and trustworthy and inform them of their appointment to ensure they are willing to take on the responsibility.

For parents with minor children, it is crucial to appoint a guardian in your will. This person should be someone you trust to raise your children in your absence. Be sure to discuss this responsibility with your chosen guardian and, if necessary, name a backup guardian.

If you wish, you can also choose to make donations to charity in your will. Many types of assets can be designated for charitable purposes, including real estate, personal property, or investments.

Authenticate the document using your own signature while in the company of a minimum of two witnesses, who will also sign your will. The chosen witnesses should not be beneficiaries, executors, or guardians mentioned within your will.

After signing your will, store it in a safe and easily accessible location, such as a fireproof safe or safe deposit box. Additionally, gather other important estate planning documents and store them in the same location. Inform your executor and loved ones of the location of these documents and how to access them.

Last Will Checklist

Last wills and testaments make sure that your wealth, assets and incomes are distributed, and any dependents provided for:

- ✓ Identify your possessions: Compile an inventory of your assets, including bank accounts, investments, real estate, personal property, and any additional valuable items you possess.
- ✓ Decide the recipients of your assets: Choose how you want your assets to be distributed and identify the beneficiaries. This could include family members, friends, or charitable organizations.
- ✓ Select an executor: opt for a reliable person to execute the terms of your will. This individual will manage your estate and guarantee that your wealth, assets, and incomes are distributed as per your directives.
- ✓ Consult an attorney: Seek guidance from an attorney with expertise in estate planning. They can provide you with information on the legal criteria for creating a will in your jurisdiction and assist you in ensuring your will complies with the law.
- ✓ Draft the will: Work with your attorney to draft the will, including details such as the beneficiaries, the executor, and how your assets will be distributed.
- ✓ Sign the will: Once the will is completed, sign it in the presence of witnesses.

✓ Store the will: Keep the original copy of your will in a safe place and inform your executor and loved ones where the will is located.

Four Ways to Write a Will

When considering the creation of a will, there are several options to choose from. This section will explore each method in detail, allowing you to make an informed decision about which approach suits your needs best:

1. Do it yourself DIY: Some individuals may choose to create their will independently using online platforms like LegalZoom. This option is cost-effective but may come with a higher risk of errors. Added to this is who works to settle an estate when you are gone.
2. Hire an attorney: This option can be more expensive, but the added expertise adds an element of confidence that your wishes will be honored. The caution here is that often the execution is still up to you.
3. Utilize a will-writing service: These services assist you in creating your will, often for a lower cost than hiring an attorney, but with more expert support than going it alone.
4. Seek a middle-ground approach: Some companies, like our office, offer a combination of DIY and professional legal services. This option provides experienced attorneys in estate planning who know their craft well with the benefit of compassionate planning to help ensure your wishes are carried out.

Estate planning is a labyrinthine process, and one has two main choices. The first choice is to do it all yourself, which means you're dedicating a significant amount of time, energy, and research to understanding complex laws and financial implications. The second choice is to hire an attorney, hoping that they have the necessary expertise to guide you through the convoluted maze of legalities.

However, there's a caveat. Often, attorneys focus solely on crafting legal documents. It's not that they're neglectful, rather, their professional responsibility is concentrated on this aspect of the process. They are not necessarily equipped or engaged to look beyond their role of documentation.

Estate planning is a multifaceted task. Beyond legal documents, prepared largely by attorneys, there are significant tax implications to consider. These financial elements often require the expertise of a Certified Public Accountant (CPA), an accountant, or an enrolled agent.

Then comes the planning piece, the task of harmonizing all these components into a cohesive whole. While attorneys specialize in crafting legal documents, they may not deal with tax issues because it's outside of their knowledge or scope. Similarly, a financial planner is limited by the boundaries of their role and cannot handle the legal documentation. The CPA, for their part, would be reluctant to meddle in legal matters or overarching planning.

This is where our business comes into play. We aim to occupy this central, integral role amidst this jumble of specialized tasks. Our mission is to coordinate, to ensure that all the puzzle pieces fit together seamlessly.

For instance, when we refer to working with an attorney to create a will, we're acknowledging that they will indeed craft the will. However, this is just a single piece of a giant puzzle. The remaining pieces — tax implications, financial planning, and coordination — can't be ignored. The risk is that someone may hire an attorney, have a will created, and then assume that they are set. But the reality is that tax considerations and overall planning are still on the table, waiting to be addressed.

This is the holistic view of estate planning we wish to stress. It's not merely about legal documentation; it's a comprehensive process that includes tax issues, financial planning, and seamless coordination of all the elements.

SIMPLE ESTATES

When a loved one passes away, their estate and bank accounts can be frozen for an extended period, putting a financial strain on the family. Here are some ways to ensure your family has enough funds to live on during this challenging time.

To help your family in this situation, consider setting up life insurance policies, as they fall outside the estate and can be paid directly to a nominated beneficiary upon death. The turnaround time for payment depends on the terms and conditions of the policy, and any necessary post-mortem examinations may cause delays.

Funeral policies are another valuable tool to ease the financial burden on your family. Whole life insurance policies and outstanding debts take time to be paid; funeral policies pay out almost immediately and cover the immediate costs associated with the funeral and burial.

If your spouse has access to your bank accounts and is the only beneficiary of your will, they will still have access but must keep detailed records of withdrawals. The executor will use this information during the distribution and liquidation process.

Joint accounts, especially for couples married in community property states, will be frozen until an executor is appointed. It is essential to discuss the handling of these accounts with your bank to understand the best course of action.

When the deceased was the sole provider, accessing funds can be challenging. However, the Administration of Estates Act allows for the release of funds for dependents and funeral expenses by approaching the High Court or the Master of the High Court.

Setting up a trust can help families circumvent many hurdles. Trusts are not frozen upon the death of a spouse, as they are dependent on the estate and not an individual. The surviving spouse, who must be a trustee, can draw from the trust as needed. However, costs and taxes are involved in setting up a trust, which should be considered.

Preparing for unexpected deaths is crucial. Ensure that vehicles and property deeds are in both spouses' names so the surviving spouse can maintain full ownership by presenting a death certificate and completing the necessary paperwork. If both spouses pass away simultaneously, the estate will go through the probate process, and an executor must be appointed.

An executor is appointed by the Master of the Court if the deceased's will does not specify one. This appointment can take anywhere from three weeks to three months.

WHAT IS PROBATE?

After a person's passing, probate is the significant legal procedure that ensues. It governs managing and redistributing the deceased's wealth—including bank accounts, property, and investments. Regardless of the presence of a will, this process is vital to ensure an orderly handling of the deceased's estate.

The executor—appointed through the will—or an administrator named without a will—manages the probate process. Their core tasks include gathering the deceased's assets, taking care of remaining debts, and distributing the residual wealth to the appropriate beneficiaries.

Key Components of Probate

Probate is a legal mechanism to assess a deceased person's wealth and determine inheritors. The focal point of probate proceedings is primarily a will's existence, authenticity, and validity. Probate can be initiated even if a will is absent. But for significantly valued estates, probate is typically obligatory. Individuals can mitigate the costs and complexities associated with the probate process by having a transparent, verifiable will or utilizing investment tools that steer clear of probate.

Deciphering the Probate Process

The probate process entails evaluating and administering assets previously held by a deceased person. After a person's death, their assets are typically examined by a probate court. The court then decides on allocating and distributing the assets to the rightful inheritors. The initial step of the probate process often involves determining if the deceased left a legal will.

Often, the departed leave documentation detailing their preferred distribution of assets post-death. However, in certain situations, a will may not be in place. These scenarios lead to unique conditions that differ based on the circumstances.

Probate with a Will

When a person leaves a will upon death, they're called a testator. Following their demise, the executor, usually a family member, starts the probate process. The will may also designate a specific executor.

The executor's obligations include filing the will with the probate court and adhering to state-specific guidelines about the filing timeframe following the decedent's death. Submitting the will sets the probate process in motion, where the court authenticates the will and formally appoints the executor. This authorization endows the executor with the legal power to act in place of the deceased.

Role of the Executor

The will typically identifies a legal representative or executor, subject to court approval. This person is responsible for locating and managing the decedent's assets and determining the estate's value according to the Internal Revenue Code (IRC).

Assets requiring probate administration usually come under the probate court's jurisdiction in the decedent's domicile at the time of death. Real estate is an exception; probate for such properties might need to occur in the counties where the property is located.

Besides handling assets, the executor's role also involves settling any taxes and debts the decedent had, using funds from the estate. Creditors typically have a limited window (around a year) from the death date to file claims against the estate for unpaid debts. Contested claims might end up in court, where a probate judge delivers the final ruling on their validity.

The executor must also file the deceased's final personal income tax returns and take care of any due estate taxes within a year from death. Once these tasks are completed, the executor seeks court approval to distribute the remaining estate assets to the beneficiaries.

Probate without a Will

When a person dies without leaving a will, it's known as dying intestate. An intestate estate is one where the deceased didn't have a will. Opting for joint ownership can help in this case. Assets jointly owned with the right of survivorship will automatically pass to the surviving joint owner upon your death, bypassing probate. This applies to real estate, bank accounts, and other types of property. It's crucial, however, to consult with an attorney or financial advisor before making such arrangements due to potential legal and financial implications.

You can designate beneficiaries on your financial accounts. This allows your retirement accounts, life insurance policies, and other financial assets to avoid probate and directly transfer to the named beneficiaries. Simply contacting the financial institution that holds the account can accomplish this.

Another method uses payable-on-death (POD) or transfer-on-death (TOD) designations. These can be applied to bank accounts, investment accounts, certain real estate types, vehicles, or other property. With a POD or TOD designation, the asset will automatically pass to the named beneficiary upon your death, sidestepping probate.

Creating a life estate might be beneficial in certain situations. It allows you to retain the right to use and enjoy the property during your lifetime while naming a beneficiary (known as a "remainderman") who will automatically inherit the property upon your death. Life estates can help avoid probate but may carry tax implications and other consequences. Therefore, it's advisable to consult with an attorney or financial advisor before setting one up.

For small estates, consider a simplified probate process. Many states offer this, significantly reducing the time and cost associated with probate. The eligibility criteria and procedures for simplified probate vary by state, so consult an attorney or local probate court to see if your estate qualifies.

Finally, maintain up-to-date estate planning documents. One of the most effective ways to minimize complications and delays during the probate process is to ensure your estate planning documents, including your will and any trusts, are current and accurately reflect your wishes. Regularly review and update your estate plan, especially following major life events like marriage, divorce, the birth of a child, or the death of a loved one.

COMMON MISTAKES MADE IN WILLS

- Failing to update the will: Your circumstances can change over time, and it's essential to update your will to reflect those changes. Failing to update your will can lead to unintended consequences, such as assets being distributed in a way you didn't intend.
- Using unclear language: It's essential to use precise language in your will to avoid confusion and ensure that your wishes are carried out. Avoid using legal jargon or vague terms that could be misinterpreted.
- Naming the wrong beneficiaries: Be sure to carefully consider whom you want to receive your assets and ensure that you have named the correct beneficiaries in your will.
- Failing to plan for contingencies: It's important to plan for contingencies in your will, such as what will happen if a beneficiary predeceases you or if your primary executor is unable to serve.
- Not considering tax implications: Depending on the size of your estate, there may be tax implications that you need to consider when creating your will. Failing to consider these implications can lead to unintended tax consequences for your heirs.

BEST OPTIONS FOR A MINOR'S INTERESTS

Estate planning is crucial, especially for those with minor children who intend to inherit assets. As a parent, it is essential to understand the various factors affecting the transfer of assets to minor beneficiaries, such as the nature of the asset, beneficiary nominations, trust structures, and legislation. To ensure that your minor children receive the inheritance you have planned for them, consider the following aspects of estate planning:

Life policies are frequently used in estate planning to guarantee that beneficiaries can access funds soon after the policyholder's death. However, South African law prohibits children under the age of 18 from directly inheriting lump sum payouts or other assets.

Retirement funds, such as pension, provident, and retirement annuity funds, involve a more complicated beneficiary nomination process, as Section 37C of the Pension Funds Act regulates the allocation of retirement fund benefits. This provision aims to ensure that the financial dependents of the deceased are not left without support. Although you may nominate your minor child as a beneficiary, the retirement fund trustees are responsible for identifying all financial dependents and determining the allocation of funds among them. Consequently, there is no guarantee that your minor child will receive the designated funds.

Tax-free savings accounts (TFSAs) allow you to nominate beneficiaries, who will receive the investment directly upon your death.

Alternatively, you can appoint a testamentary trust as the beneficiary of the TFSA.

In the case of local and offshore unit trust investments, you cannot appoint beneficiaries directly, as the proceeds become part of your estate and are distributed according to your will. These proceeds are subject to estate duty and executor's fees.

Minor children can inherit immovable property with the assistance of their legal guardian. However, potential risks include insufficient liquidity in the estate and limited authority of the guardian over the asset. To mitigate these risks, consider bequeathing fixed property to a testamentary trust.

For personal belongings, you wish to leave to your minor children, draft a letter of wishes that clearly describes each item, its location, and any identifying features. This will help avoid confusion and ensure your children receive the intended items.

The best options for looking after a minor's interests after your death. Providing for and protecting a minor child after your death is an important consideration when creating a will or estate plan. Here are some steps you can take to ensure that your child is taken care of:

- Choose a guardian: In your will, you can name a guardian for your child.
- Create a trust: You can set up a trust to provide for your child financially. The trust can be managed by a trustee who will distribute the funds according to your wishes.

- Name a trustee: This person will be responsible for managing the funds and making distributions to provide for your child's needs.
- Consider life insurance: The proceeds from the policy can be used to support your child's needs and cover any expenses related to their care.
- Leave specific instructions: It's important to leave specific instructions in your will about how you want your child to be taken care of. This can include instructions about their education, medical care, and other important aspects of their upbringing.

HOW TO PROVIDE FOR A SPECIAL NEEDS CHILD

It's essential to develop an estate plan to ensure the security and well-being of your child in the event of your death or incapacitation. The task may seem daunting, but by breaking it down into smaller steps, you can create a comprehensive plan that covers all your bases.

1. Get organized: Compile important personal information and documents for both you and your child, such as Social Security numbers, Medicare information, and relevant legal documents. Keep these organized in a file cabinet or digitally stored in a secure location.
2. Document medical history: Compile information about medical providers, medications, allergies, and insurance coverage for both you and your child. Include details about your child's education and support services.

3. Record financial information: Create a chart detailing income source, asset values, beneficiary designations, and contact information for financial advisors.

4. Secure online accounts and passwords: Compile a list of usernames, passwords, and security answers for online accounts, and store them securely.

5. Compose a letter of intent: Being the parent of a child with disabilities, it's important to prepare a document that clearly communicates your precise wishes regarding your child's care and support.

6. Prepare for your child's future: Think about how you want to cater to your child's needs if you are no longer able to care for them. Hold conversations on these matters with friends, family members, and professionals to make well-informed decisions.

7. Seek advice from a special needs lawyer: Engage with a legal professional specializing in special needs planning to create essential legal documents and establish financial strategies, such as special needs trusts.

8. Prepare for your own potential incapacity or disability: Decide on how your financial and health care affairs will be managed if you're unable to do so. Explore different options like informal arrangements, powers of attorney, and health care directives.

9. Review your child's guardianship or conservatorship: Determine who should succeed in managing your child's financial and health care decisions and ensure that the necessary legal processes are in place.

10. Plan for end-of-life arrangements: Decide on organ and tissue donation preferences and make funeral plans for both you and your child.

11. Update your plan regularly: Revisit your estate plan as circumstances change and consult with an attorney when updates are needed.

PROTECTING AND PROVIDING FOR A SPOUSE

How to best protect and provide for a remaining spouse:

- Bequeath assets to your spouse: Within your will, you can pass on assets to your spouse, including monetary resources, property, and investments. This action ensures they have adequate support following your demise.
- Contemplate establishing a trust: Setting up a trust for your spouse is a prudent way to provide for their financial needs upon your death. A designated trustee will manage the trust, who will distribute the funds based on your stipulations.
- Designate your spouse as a beneficiary: Assign your spouse as the recipient of your life insurance policies, retirement funds, and other assets. This assignment ensures they acquire the funds directly, sidestepping the probate process.
- Consider joint ownership: If property ownership is shared with your spouse, it will automatically be transferred to them upon your demise.

- Regularly assess and modify your plan: Regular evaluation and necessary adjustments are crucial to ensure it mirrors your current desires and situations.

How do you secure yourself as the remaining spouse?

First and foremost, ensure that your partner has a will that includes you. Ensure that the executor of the will understands your situation and will be sensitive to your needs. If your partner has a family from a previous marriage, this becomes even more critical to avoid feelings of being second-best or overlooked during the grieving process.

Examine your partner's beneficiary designations, as these determine where their assets will go upon death. Your partner must name you as a beneficiary on life insurance policies and bank accounts, ensuring you have quick access to funds for bills and other necessities.

A cohabitation agreement is another essential document to consider. This contract can give you the right to remain in the home you shared with your partner in the event of their passing. This is particularly helpful if you contribute to household expenses, as it will allow you to maintain some semblance of stability during an incredibly challenging time.

Joint ownership of property is another way to secure your future. If your partner adds your name to the deed of their home, you will automatically inherit the property upon their death. However, ensure you have enough financial resources to maintain the property afterward.

Taking care of minor children is of utmost importance. If you share children with your partner, they must provide for them, as well as any children from previous relationships. If your partner has an ex-spouse, their divorce agreement might require them to maintain life insurance for alimony and child support. It's essential to address these matters ahead of time to avoid potential conflicts.

Review your partner's healthcare proxy, ensuring you have the legal right to visit them, consult with their doctors, and make medical decisions if they are hospitalized. Without this designation, you might be excluded from crucial decisions by other family members.

Lastly, discuss your partner's wishes regarding the handling of their remains. As morbid as this topic may seem, it is essential to address it to avoid disputes with other family members. Please make certain that their intentions are documented in writing and in accordance with state law, typically within their will.

Protecting your estate from a claim by a spouse.

Protecting your estate from a claim by a spouse is essential, especially if you are separated but not yet divorced. To ensure that your property, finances, and children are protected and provided for in case of death or moving forward with your new, single life, it is crucial to consider several factors.

First, assess whether you have made a formal financial settlement for a clean break. This step is vital, as it helps avoid future claims from your ex-spouse. Also, review your will to ensure it does not leave everything to your ex-spouse or grant them control over your estate through a Lasting Power of Attorney.

Examine how your property is owned and whether you have updated your life insurance and pension beneficiaries. Reflect on whether you were treated fairly during the separation process and whether your spouse passed away without untangling your finances.

Separated couples should be aware of the risks involved in not getting a divorce. These risks include having no control over your spouse's finances, becoming estranged, changing circumstances for better or worse, meeting new partners, and potential financial provisions. It is crucial to protect yourself and your estate from these risks.

There are several ways to protect yourself and your estate from a claim by a spouse:

1. Get a divorce and financial order: This step legally ends the marriage and fairly divides the couple's assets. A financial order from the court will terminate any future claims between the two parties, often referred to as a 'clean break.'
2. Separation agreement: If you are undecided about getting a divorce or the timing is not right, a separation agreement can provide clarity. It outlines financial arrangements, living arrangements, and responsibilities related to children. Although not legally binding, courts will likely uphold such agreements if adequately negotiated, fair, and meet both parties' financial needs.
3. Pre-nuptial or post-nuptial agreement: These agreements can help protect your estate if you separate. They outline how assets will be divided in case of a separation.

4. Make or update your will: Ensure that the correct person makes your assets and decisions about your estate. Update your will to reflect your new circumstances and include a letter of wishes to explain your situation. It is crucial to rewrite your will if you are in a new relationship but not yet divorced.

Death and Taxes in America

In finance, when an individual's assets are passed on to their beneficiaries, federal estate taxes come into play.

It's important to remember that these numbers don't affect most estates. Yet, if you foresee your estate outpacing these limits, you must arm yourself with a proactive plan, possibly seeking guidance from a seasoned financial advisor for advanced estate planning.

Numerous states impose their own estate taxes. If you're a resident of one of these states, you may be subject to both federal and state estate taxes.

The IRS has introduced an estate tax deduction to counteract the double taxing of assets. This mechanism permits the deduction of the estate tax paid on Income in Respect of a Decedent (IRD) from the income tax due on the same IRD.

If you're worried about estate taxes diminishing your beneficiaries' inheritance, consider investigating strategies to limit your tax exposure.

Upon an individual's death in the U.S., the tax landscape might include:

1. Estate tax: The Estate Tax is a tax on your right to transfer property at your death. It must begin with an accounting of everything you own or have interests in at the date of your passing.

2. Inheritance tax: Only a few states impose an inheritance tax, which is a tax on assets transferred to heirs. The tax rates and regulations differ from state to state.

3. Income tax: Should the deceased person have generated income in their year of death, their estate might need to file a final income tax return and settle any taxes owed. Should the estate earn income following the individual's demise, it might be obligated to file an estate income tax return and pay taxes on this income.

4. Gift tax: If the deceased person made significant gifts while alive, their estate might be subject to gift taxes on those gifts.

HOW CAN WE REDUCE OUR TAX BURDEN?

Proper utilization of these strategies can help mitigate the effects of estate taxes and aid in securing your family's financial future.

Put your funds in a retirement annuity: The Pension Funds Act governs Retirement Annuities (RAs), which offer substantial tax benefits to investors. The assets within RAs do not contribute to your deceased estate, thus not factoring into the computation of your estate tax obligation or executor's fees. This means your RA continues to provide tax advantages even posthumously, with the distribution of funds to your financial dependents at the discretion of the fund trustees.

Strategically use life insurance: Designating your surviving spouse as the recipient of your domestic life insurance policy ensures that the proceeds are paid directly to them upon your demise, bypassing your deceased estate and dodging estate tax and executor's fees. Life insurance can also be employed to cover any estate tax obligation without needing to liquidate assets intended for your heirs. For this, you would need to designate your estate as the policy beneficiary.

Make the most of your donations tax exemptions: If you've established a living trust, you can further reduce your estate tax obligation by utilizing your annual tax exemption. Nonetheless, avoid donating capital you may require for living expenses, as once it's given to the trust, it comes under the trustees' control.

Establish a testamentary trust for your underage children: To ensure the effective management of assets intended for your underage children's benefit, contemplate setting up a testamentary trust. By naming this trust as the recipient of assets in your will, the assets are directly transferred to the trust upon your demise. This strategy sidesteps potential complications due to the legal inability of minor children to inherit and prevents unwanted situations such as the state-operated Guardian's Fund managing their funds.

As demonstrated, multiple tools are at your disposal to limit the impact of estate taxes on your loved ones. However, it's crucial to consider these tactics not individually but as components of a broader tax planning scheme.

HOW TO CREATE A TANK-LIKE TRUST

When it comes to estate planning, trusts are multifaceted instruments designed to possess and oversee assets on behalf of beneficiaries. They offer benefits such as safeguarding assets, minimizing taxes, and enabling smooth wealth transition.

Trusts can serve various purposes, like ensuring financial support for minor children, shielding assets from creditors, or guaranteeing proper asset management for individuals with special needs.

Here's how you can set up a trust that matches your needs:

Identify the type of trust you need: Many trust types exist, each catering to a distinct purpose. Your choice of trust depends on your specific objectives and circumstances. For example, a revocable living trust allows you to make alterations or dissolve the trust during your lifetime, whereas an irrevocable trust cannot be modified once formed.

Select a trustee: The trustee is vital in managing the trust and allocating its assets according to your wishes. Your trustee could be a family member, a friend, or a professional trustee like a bank or trust company. Choosing a responsible, reliable person who can handle the responsibilities linked with trust administration is crucial.

Draft the trust document: This legal paper details the terms of the trust, including the trustee's obligations, the beneficiaries, and the distribution of assets. A knowledgeable attorney can assist you in composing a comprehensive trust document that accurately represents your wishes and adheres to the relevant laws.

Fund the trust: To operationalize the trust, you must transfer assets. These assets could include cash, investments, and real estate. The process of funding the trust depends on the kind of assets involved, and properly completing this step is vital to ensuring the trust operates as planned.

Sign and notarize the trust document: The trust becomes legally binding once you sign and notarize the document. Notarization entails a notary public verifying the identities of the signatories and witnessing their signatures, adding an additional safeguard against possible legal disputes.

Regularly review and update the trust: It's crucial to review and update your trust periodically to make sure it remains in line with your changing wishes and circumstances. Changes in your family dynamics, financial situation, or relevant laws might require modifications to the trust terms.

STEP-BY-STEP WILL PLANNING CHECKLIST

Here is a comprehensive will planning checklist with different options to consider:

1. Explore your options: DIY (online sites such as LegalZoom.com or Trustsandwills.com, for example), hiring an estate planning attorney, or finding a service that combines both, such as our office.
2. Determine your beneficiaries, naming primary and contingent recipients.
3. Consider including special bequests like charitable donations or gifts to specific individuals.

4. Choose an executor and obtain their agreement to serve in this role.
5. Appoint guardians for minor children and get their consent, considering primary and alternate guardians.
6. State your preferences for burial or cremation and any specific funeral or memorial service instructions.
7. Review and revise your will draft, ensuring clarity and accuracy. Consult with an attorney if necessary.
8. Sign your will in front of at least two witnesses (or three, depending on state requirements) who are not beneficiaries. Witnesses should also sign to confirm your soundness of mind.
9. Securely store your will and inform your executor, close family members, and attorney of its location.

These are the essential steps to create a thorough and effective last will and testament. Be sure to keep your will updated as relationships and life circumstances change.

CHAPTER SUMMARY

When acting toward estate planning and wealth preservation, it's essential to remember that other intangible aspects of your legacy are just as vital to consider. These include cherished memories, treasured family traditions, valuable life lessons, and more. These intangible assets are an integral part of what makes you who you are and deserve to be preserved and passed down to future generations.

Document your personal and family history: Your personal story and your family's history are significant parts of your legacy. Consider writing an autobiography, compiling a family tree, or creating a collection of family anecdotes to share with future generations. These accounts will help preserve your memories and provide your descendants with a richer understanding of their roots and heritage.

Establish meaningful family traditions: Family traditions play a crucial role in fostering a sense of belonging and continuity among generations. Be intentional in cultivating traditions that reflect your values and can be passed down to your children and grandchildren. These might include annual gatherings, holiday celebrations, or unique rituals that become treasured family memories.

Share your wisdom and life lessons: You have accumulated a wealth of knowledge and experiences that can be invaluable to your loved ones. Consider writing a series of letters, creating a video or audio recording, or crafting a personal blog to share your insights, advice, and reflections on life. These resources can serve as inspiration and guidance for your descendants as they navigate their life journeys.

Preserve your family's cultural heritage: Your family's cultural background is essential to your legacy. Actively preserve and share your cultural traditions, customs, languages, and stories with your children and grandchildren. This can involve teaching them traditional recipes, passing on heirlooms, or sharing the history of their ancestors. In doing so, you help ensure that your family's cultural identity remains vibrant and alive for generations.

Encourage your children and grandchildren to participate in charitable activities, volunteer work, or community service.

Establishing a family foundation or setting up a donor-advised fund can also enable your family to carry on your legacy of giving.

Foster strong family bonds and communication: Open, honest communication is the foundation of strong family relationships. Encourage regular family meetings, dinners, or gatherings where members can share their thoughts, feelings, and experiences. These connections will serve as the backbone of your family's legacy, ensuring that future generations remain close-knit and supportive of one another.

While the financial aspects of estate planning are undoubtedly crucial, the intangible elements of your legacy should not be overlooked. Preserving and sharing your memories, traditions, wisdom, and values with your loved ones helps create a lasting impact that transcends material wealth. Remember that your legacy is not just about the assets you leave behind but also the stories, values, and connections that shape your family's future.

MAKE A DIFFERENCE WITH YOUR BOOK REVIEW:

I'm happy you have this book in hand to discover what the wealthy and savvy do differently when it comes to estate planning. But here's the thing – we're not just on a journey for ourselves. We're on a mission to make a difference in the lives of others, too.

Picture this: Someone out there, just like you or maybe a version of yourself from the past, is seeking guidance on estate planning. They're eager to make a positive impact but might be feeling overwhelmed and unsure where to begin.

That's where your book review comes in. By sharing your thoughts on *Estate Planning 101 - What The Wealthy & Savvy Do Differently*, you're not just helping me; you're helping countless others who need direction.

Your review could be the catalyst for someone to finally take control of their affairs, provide for their loved ones, or fulfill their philanthropic dreams. And the best part? It only takes a minute of your time.

So, will you help me empower others by leaving a review? Your words have the power to change lives, and together, we can make a real difference.

Ready to make a difference? Just scan the QR code

Or go to, https://notaxs.me/101

PART 2: NON-TANGIBLE WEALTH

CHAPTER FIVE

PRESERVING YOUR LEGACY & LIFE LESSONS

We are a continuum. Just as we reach back to our ancestors for our fundamental values, so we, as guardians of that legacy, must reach ahead to our children and their children. And we do so with a sense of sacredness in that reaching. – Paul Tsongas

THE IMPORTANCE OF PASSING DOWN A LEGACY

A legacy is a precious gift that we pass down to future generations. It encompasses our life experiences, beliefs, values, and traditions, shaping the lives of those who come after us. Leaving a meaningful legacy is essential because it is a guiding light for future generations, preserving memories, teaching life lessons, and inspiring greatness.

Living Your Legacy by Example

The most powerful way to leave a legacy is to live by example. Demonstrating kindness, honesty, and hard work in everyday life has a far more significant impact than simply telling your children or loved ones about these values. By standing up for what you believe in, even in challenging situations, you instill in them the power of conviction. Pursuing your passions and dreams purposefully teaches them the significance of living a fulfilling life. Embodying kindness and compassion, even towards those who may not deserve it, helps them understand the true meaning of character. Living your legacy daily ensures that it will be carried forward by the people you influence.

Making Each Day Count

How you live each day is more critical than your accomplishments. Your attitudes and actions create your legacy. Approaching each day with gratitude, enthusiasm, and kindness will leave a positive, lasting impact on others. People will remember how you made them feel rather than the specifics of your accomplishments. Living each day with compassion and joy ensures that your legacy will uplift and inspire others.

The Power of Love

Love is a potent emotion that can strengthen, comfort, and bring joy to our lives. Sharing love with others is one of our most significant gifts. We create lasting, supportive relationships by expressing love and commitment to family and friends. Demonstrating love and passion for our work cultivates a positive, productive environment. Showing love and respect for all people, regardless of background or beliefs, contributes to a more just and peaceful world.

Journaling for the Future

Keeping a journal may seem daunting, but it is invaluable to future generations. Documenting key events, conversations, and thoughts provides a unique glimpse into your life, helping to preserve your memories and legacy. Journals offer a space to process emotions and experiences while creating a cherished record for those who come after you.

Strengthening Family Bonds

Family is vital to our lives, providing unwavering support and understanding. Being open and honest with your family about your values and experiences helps create a stronger bond. Sharing stories from your past and present helps your family understand you better and fosters a more loving environment. Remember that spending quality time together and creating shared experiences are more valuable than material gifts.

Honesty, Transparency, and Effective Communication

Building lasting relationships and leaving a solid legacy requires honest and transparent communication. These qualities foster trust and respect, allowing for deeper connections with others. Honesty in communication leaves a transparent and memorable legacy, appreciated by those who knew you.

Living for Others Through Service and Connection

One of the most selfless acts is living for others. Serving humanity or those closest to us has a positive impact not only on their lives but also on our own. Sharing our vision and values with our loved ones creates a sense of connection and belonging that is more valuable than any material possession.

Ground Your Actions in the Larger Picture of Truth

Connecting our actions with principles and purposes more significant than ourselves is essential. Doing so creates a lasting story that transcends individual experiences and connects us to something more significant. This approach to life imbues our actions with meaning and purpose, shaping a story worth telling and contributing to a better world.

WRITE THEM DOWN

One of the simplest ways to preserve family traditions and stories is to write them down. You can create a family photo/history book, write personal memoirs or a family journal, or record your stories and memories using audio or video.

When writing a memoir, you're taking your readers on an exhilarating ride through a powerful and transformative story. To create a compelling memoir, it's essential to understand and utilize certain elements that make this genre unique.

Narrow your focus: Unlike an autobiography, a memoir is a snapshot of a theme or two from your life. By narrowing down your focus, you'll be able to offer readers a deeper understanding of a specific experience or aspect of your life. Use a timeline to identify the turning points in your life and choose the ones with the most emotional or thematic resonance.

Include more than just your story: While your memoir is primarily about your own experiences, providing a broader context is essential. This might involve sharing intimate moments, challenges, or aspects of your relationships with others. For example, if a prominent figure like Kamala Harris were to write a memoir, she might include anecdotes about juggling her career, marriage, and family life.

Tell the truth: A powerful memoir requires honesty and authenticity. It's essential to be truthful, even if it means potentially upsetting the people in your life. For example, Shannon Hernandez's memoir, "Breaking the Silence: My Final Forty Days as a Public School Teacher," offers a brutally honest account of her challenges in the education system.

Showcase your personal growth: A memoir should demonstrate how you have grown, changed, or transformed due to your experiences. Showing how you evolved as a person throughout your story will make your memoir more meaningful and impactful for your readers.

To gather inspiration for your memoir, consider reading examples from various categories like structured memoirs, thematic memoirs, and memoirs with solid takeaways. For instance, structured memoirs like Kiese Laymon's "Heavy" or Lori Gottleib's "Maybe You Should Talk to Someone" can teach you about organizing your story. Thematic memoirs, like Roxane Gay's "Hunger: A Memoir of (My Body)" or Gabrielle Hamilton's "Blood, Bones, and Butter," can help you explore the themes that drive your narrative. Lastly, memoirs with strong takeaways, such as Elizabeth Gilbert's "Eat, Pray, Love," show how to create moments of reflection and connection with your readers.

SHARE THEM WITH FAMILY MEMBERS

Sharing family traditions and stories with younger generations can help keep them alive. Consider hosting family gatherings where older family members can share stories and pass on important life lessons to younger members.

There are countless ways to establish family traditions, and every family can create their own unique rituals that best suit their individual needs and values. Here are five suggestions for creating family traditions that will bring your family closer together.

Traditions of Daily Family Life

Establishing daily rituals can help strengthen family bonds and create a sense of routine and stability. Bedtime rituals, such as reading, snuggling, and saying prayers together, offer a time for parents and children to unwind and bond at the end of the day. Another option is setting aside time for one-on-one activities with each child, like having dinner together or engaging in a shared hobby. This allows parents to focus on each child's unique qualities and fosters individual connections. Additionally, holding weekly family meetings over a favorite meal can provide a forum for discussing schedules, airing differences, and planning for upcoming family events.

Example: A family might choose to have a weekly pizza and game night, where everyone takes turns choosing a board game to play after dinner.

Annual Family Days

Planning special outings or events throughout the year can create lasting memories and bring the family together in a spirit of fun and adventure. Annual family days might include a camping trip, fishing excursion, or the first baseball game of the season. These events can be eagerly anticipated and involve cooperative planning and preparation. Other options include a yearly "spring cleaning" day, where the entire family works together to spruce up the house, or volunteering in the community on a regular basis.

Example: A family could plan an annual trip to a local amusement park or set aside one day each month for volunteer work at a nearby animal shelter.

The Annual Family Vacation

Family vacations provide a chance to explore new places, bond over shared experiences, and create lifelong memories. They can range from relaxing beach getaways to educational trips to historical sites. It is essential that each family member has a say in choosing the destination or the theme of the trip, whether it be an eco-adventure, a farm or ranch stay, or a service trip to help a community in need.

Example: One year, a family might decide to explore their ancestral homeland, tracing their roots and learning about their cultural heritage.

Another year, they might embark on a road trip to visit national parks nationwide.

Family Traditions that Connect Us to Our Past

Honoring and remembering ancestors is an essential aspect of many family traditions. Visiting gravesites, making trips to ancestral homelands, or incorporating inherited objects into family ceremonies can create a sense of continuity and cultural identity. These traditions help families explore their heritage and establish connections with previous generations.

Example: A family with Irish ancestry might choose to celebrate St. Patrick's Day by cooking a traditional Irish meal, listening to Irish music, and sharing stories about their ancestors.

Holiday Traditions

Holidays and special occasions provide ample opportunities to establish family traditions. Birthdays, anniversaries, and religious or national celebrations can be marked by unique family rituals, like preparing a favorite meal, visiting a special place, or participating in community events. Exploring and participating in the holidays and traditions of other cultures can also foster understanding, acceptance, and appreciation for diversity.

Example: A family might choose to celebrate the winter holidays by inviting friends and neighbors to a festive potluck dinner, where everyone brings a dish from their cultural background.

USE TECHNOLOGY

Technology can be a valuable tool for preserving family traditions and stories. You can use digital tools like family websites, social media, and cloud storage to store and share photos, videos, and other digital content.

Throughout history, families have sought ways to capture and preserve their memories. As technology has advanced, our methods of documenting family life have evolved, making it easier and more accessible to preserve precious moments for future generations. Here are the various tools and technologies revolutionizing how we document our family history.

Digital Cameras

The invention of digital cameras transformed the way we take and store photographs. Since the first consumer digital camera became available in 1994, these devices have become smaller, faster, and more affordable. Today, many smartphones have built-in cameras with better quality than early digital cameras, making it effortless to capture and share family memories instantly.

High-Definition Video

Initially, video cameras were bulky, heavy, and produced low-quality images. Over time, they have evolved into lightweight, portable devices capable of recording high-definition videos. Many smartphones now come equipped with high-definition video cameras, making it easier and more affordable for families to document important events such as weddings, graduations, and birthdays.

Example: Parents can now capture their child's school play in stunning high-definition video, preserving the memory in vivid detail for years to come.

Digital Picture Frames

Digital picture frames offer a modern solution for high-resolution family photos. These devices function as small storage and playback systems, allowing you to load and display your favorite digital images in a traditional picture frame. With customizable playback rates and transition settings, digital picture frames provide a dynamic and visually appealing way to showcase your family memories.

Example: Load a digital picture frame with cherished family vacation photos and set it on your coffee table for visitors to enjoy as they flip through the changing images.

Video and Photo Conversion

Many families have accumulated vast collections of printed photos, negatives, slides, and even old film reels. Converting these memories into digital formats allows for more accessible storage, preservation, and sharing. While some tasks, such as scanning photos, can be done at home, others may require professional assistance, such as converting VHS tapes or film reels to digital formats.

Example: Convert your grandparents' old wedding video from VHS to a digital format, ensuring that future generations can witness and cherish this special moment in your family's history.

Cloud Storage

While digital technology has made storing and sharing family memories easier, it also poses the risk of losing precious files due to accidental deletion or hard drive crashes. Cloud storage provides a solution by allowing you to store your digital files securely online. Many services offer unlimited storage for a monthly fee, ensuring that your family's most treasured memories are safe and accessible whenever you have an internet connection.

Example: Use cloud storage to back up your entire family photo collection so you can easily access and share your memories from any device, even if your computer crashes or your smartphone is lost.

CREATE A LEGACY PLAN

The legacy and estate planning journey can initially seem like a mission to maximize the wealth you bequeath to your family and favorite charities while reducing tax obligations. But a genuinely impactful legacy extends beyond monetary wealth—it also encompasses preparing your family for the responsibilities accompanying wealth inheritance.

Drawing from my experience working with affluent families, I've observed that a holistic approach—one that blends financial literacy for emerging generations with a cross-generational comprehension of the family's values and views regarding wealth—is most effective. In pursuit of this, consider examining these three fundamental questions.

What intentions does the family have for the created wealth?

The initial step in crafting a legacy plan involves recognizing your goals. These could encompass immediate cash flow necessities, long-term wealth transfer strategies, or multi-generational philanthropic ambitions. Transparent and sincere dialogues with family members and trusted advisors can help bring these goals into focus. Excellent communication fosters the trust necessary to seamlessly transition your legacy across generational lines.

For instance: A family might choose to channel their wealth towards supporting local community initiatives, providing scholarships for disadvantaged students, or investing in ecologically sustainable businesses.

How can I intertwine values and wealth to forge a durable legacy?

Identifying your family's core values is pivotal to formulating a significant legacy. Contemplate the causes that are closest to your heart, such as local issues or charity organizations you aim to back. Engaging your loved ones in discussions can assist you in crafting a wealth plan that resonates with your values and aspirations.

For instance: A family with a deep-rooted dedication to environmental preservation might decide to weave this value into their legacy by funding green initiatives, backing eco-friendly businesses, or setting up a nature reserve under their name.

Is my legacy plan synchronized with my vision?

Your legacy plan should resonate with your values, objectives, and overarching investment approach. Begin by examining your current wealth plan to pinpoint changes required to align it with your vision. Successful families often follow two best practices: shaping family wealth objectives and collaborating with advisors to pinpoint the most efficacious strategies for realizing those goals. Engaging strategies with multiple specialists can prove advantageous as they can tackle different yet interlinked issues.

For instance: A family might harbor a vision of fostering future generations through education. By aligning their legacy plan with this vision, they can create college funds for their grandchildren or donate to a professorship at a university under their family's name.

CONSIDER POWER OF PHILANTHROPY 101

A legacy plan is a roadmap for passing on your values, beliefs, and traditions to future generations. It can include instructions for how to preserve and share your family's history and traditions, as well as guidelines for passing on your assets and philanthropic values.

As we explore the history and current state of philanthropy, it's crucial to understand the successes, failures, and the evolving landscape of philanthropic efforts. One useful resource for examining some of the highest-achieving foundation initiatives is the Casebook for The Foundation: A Great American Secret, which discusses 100 cases since 1900. Despite some limitations and biases, the Casebook provides valuable insights into the nature of philanthropic work and its impact.

Philanthropy has an impressive track record, particularly in the areas of research (especially medical), healthcare, and education. Foundations have often led the way in these fields, achieving tangible results that have significantly improved lives. Some of the most notable accomplishments include building schools and hospitals in rural areas, advocating for federal legislation in various sectors, and funding major medical advances.

Over time, however, the space for doing good has become more crowded, and the most impressive achievements seem to belong to earlier eras. This could be because government spending on health and education has increased substantially over the years, leaving fewer opportunities for philanthropic organizations to make a significant impact.

Additionally, the focus of philanthropy has evolved. Historically, foundations often commissioned blue-ribbon panels to produce reports on various topics or piloted programs that later became government initiatives. Today, the approach to philanthropy is more diverse, but there seems to be less variety in terms of tactics and theories of change.

When examining why philanthropy was needed in certain cases, some common situations emerge. Often, the primary beneficiaries were disadvantaged people or the environment, who couldn't create change for themselves. Many projects also focus on funding research or improving education, which can have a weak connection between investment and reward. Other cases included efforts to educate the public on health, advocate for government support, or facilitate international coordination.

Despite the valuable insights offered by the Casebook, its limitations include a lack of "failure stories" and dissenting perspectives, an overemphasis on large foundations, and a focus on innovation rather than results. To gain a more comprehensive understanding of the history of philanthropy, it is necessary to explore additional resources and perspectives.

Anyone Can Be A Philanthropist: A Guide to Smart Giving

Philanthropy is not a privilege restricted to the upper crust of society. With a touch of planning and commitment, anyone can create a ripple in others' lives by donating their time, skills, or monetary assets.

STORIES

In America, there's a notable culture of giving back, with affluent individuals frequently contributing monetary aid to communities and causes in need. Nonetheless, philanthropy isn't confined to the rich—everyone has the potential to effect positive change in the lives of others.

Understanding a Philanthropist

A philanthropist is an individual who bestows their money, wisdom, time, capabilities, or aptitudes to aid others and forge a better world. While philanthropists are often stereotypically depicted as millionaires with sizeable donations, the truth is, that anyone can be a philanthropist, regardless of their financial status.

The Advantages of Being a Philanthropist

The principal advantage of being a philanthropist is the fulfillment of some of our deepest human desires, like certainty, significance, diversity, love/connection, growth, and giving back. As motivational speaker Tony Robbins often notes, "It's not what we receive, but who we become and what we give that infuses our lives with purpose."

Noteworthy Philanthropists

Here are a few examples of renowned philanthropists impacting the world:

Paul Tudor Jones: This hedge fund magnate established the Robin Hood Foundation focusing on education and alleviating poverty, serving families in New York for over three decades.

Ray Dalio: The founder of Bridgewater Associates, Ray Dalio, alongside his family, has donated over $1 billion since 2003 to a myriad of meaningful causes through Dalio Philanthropies.

Michael Jordan: The iconic NBA player has donated millions to various causes, including Friends of the Children, Hurricane Florence relief efforts, and the establishment of new medical clinics in his native town.

Serena Williams: The tennis legend established The Yetunde Price Resource Center in Compton and channels proceeds from her daughter's clothing sales to the Williams Sisters Fund for violence prevention in urban areas.

Chapter Summary

You can make sure you will be remembered in several ways, and one of the most impactful methods is through philanthropy. By dedicating your time, talents, and resources to making a positive change in the world, you can leave a legacy that speaks to your values and passions. Here are various ways to create a lasting impact through philanthropic endeavors.

Establish a foundation!

One way to leave a lasting legacy is by establishing a foundation in your name or in honor of a loved one.

Endowments and scholarships.

Another way to make a lasting impact is by creating an endowment or scholarship fund to support a specific cause, institution, or group of individuals. Endowments can be established at universities, museums, or other nonprofit organizations, providing a perpetual funding source for a particular program or cause. Scholarships, on the other hand, can provide financial assistance to deserving students, enabling them to pursue their educational goals. For example, the Rhodes Scholarship, established in 1902 by Cecil Rhodes, has supported thousands of scholars from around the world in their pursuit of higher education at the University of Oxford.

Naming opportunities.

Naming opportunities offer another way to create a lasting legacy. By making a significant donation to a nonprofit organization or institution, you may be able to have a building, program, or initiative named in your honor. This can serve as a lasting reminder of your commitment to a particular cause or institution. An example of this is the David Geffen School of Medicine at UCLA, named in recognition of a $200 million donation from entertainment mogul David Geffen.

Planned giving.

Planned giving is another avenue for leaving a lasting legacy. This can include bequests in your will, charitable remainder trusts, or charitable lead trusts. For instance, Chuck Feeney, the founder of the Atlantic Philanthropies, has made numerous planned gifts to various educational institutions and other nonprofits, ensuring that his philanthropic legacy continues long after his passing.

Volunteer and leadership roles.

Your legacy is not solely defined by financial contributions. By dedicating your time and talents to a cause you are passionate about, you can make a significant impact and be remembered for your commitment and leadership. Serving on a nonprofit board, mentoring others, or taking on leadership roles within an organization can leave a lasting impression and inspire others to follow in your footsteps. For example, the late Congressman and civil rights leader John Lewis devoted his life to fighting for social justice and inspired countless others through his activism and leadership.

Creating a lasting legacy through philanthropy involves a combination of financial contributions, strategic planning, and personal commitment. By pursuing these various avenues, you can ensure that your passions, values, and dedication to making a difference in the world are remembered for generations to come.

CHAPTER SIX

LEAVING YOUR MARK

That is your legacy on this Earth when you leave this Earth: how many hearts you touched.

- Patti Davis

YOU CAN CREATE A CHARITABLE FOUNDATION

You can create a charitable foundation or donate to causes you care about, such as education, healthcare, the environment, or social justice.

It's an opportunity to give back to the community, create a lasting legacy, and make a real impact in the lives of others. However, with numerous charities to choose from, it can be challenging to determine which organization aligns with your values and goals. Here are four key questions to consider when deciding which charity to support through your estate plan.

Question #1: *Which charitable cause resonates with you?*

When selecting a charity, it's essential to identify the cause that you feel most passionate about. Charitable organizations cover a wide array of areas, from environmental conservation to humanitarian aid. Reflect on the issues that matter most to you, whether it's providing education for underprivileged children, supporting cancer research, or preserving wildlife habitats. By choosing a charity that aligns with your passion, you'll ensure your estate's contributions make a meaningful impact.

For example, suppose you have always been passionate about providing clean water to needy communities. In that case, you might support a charity like Charity Water, which focuses on bringing safe drinking water to people in developing countries.

Question #2: *Which charity organizations are you familiar with?*

After determining the cause you're most passionate about, start researching charities that work in that area. Begin with organizations you're already familiar with or have heard about from friends and family. These recommendations can be a valuable starting point when evaluating different charities. As you research, compare each organization's mission, values, and impact to determine the best fit for your estate plan.

For instance, if you're interested in supporting education, you might already be familiar with organizations like UNICEF, which works to improve children's lives worldwide or *Teach for America*, which focuses on educational equity in the United States.

Question #3: *How transparent is the organization about its financials and impact?*

When choosing a charity, it's crucial to understand how they allocate funds and what impact they've made with previous donations.

Reputable organizations should provide transparent financial information, including administrative costs and how much money goes directly toward programs and services. They should also share measurable outcomes of their work, such as the number of lives positively impacted, or the amount of funding allocated to specific projects.

For example, if you're considering donating to a food bank, you might want to know the percentage of funds used for purchasing and distributing food compared to administrative costs. Transparency in these areas will help you feel confident that your donation is being used effectively.

Question #4: *What is the charity's reputation, and how do they treat their donors?*

A charity's reputation and approach to donor relations are essential factors to consider. How organizations respond to inquiries and whether they're forthcoming with information or evasive. If a charity pressures or guilts you into donating, that may be a red flag. Additionally, investigate what others say about the charity by reading reviews and social media comments. This can provide valuable insight into the organization's credibility and donor satisfaction.

For example, suppose you're considering supporting a local animal shelter. In that case, you might look at online reviews to gauge the community's opinion of their work and how they treat animals and donors.

<u>Starting a charity foundation</u>

If you are considering starting a private foundation or finding alternative ways to support social causes you care about, it is crucial to understand the different options available. This section will help you explore private foundations, setting one up, and donor-advised funds as an alternative philanthropic vehicle.

Deciphering Private Foundations

A private foundation is a standalone legal entity that dispenses grants originating from its charitable investments. Typically, these investments are sourced from a single individual, a family, a corporation, or a restricted list of such sources. The foundation is operated by its chosen trustees or directors and is recognized by the IRS as a tax-exempt 501(c)(3) entity. In contrast to public charities, private foundations do not solicit or receive funds from the public.

Donor-Advised Funds

(DAFs) provide a more straightforward alternative to private foundations. These vehicles for giving allow you to experience the perks of a private foundation without administrative obligations. Establishing a donor-advised fund is typically less expensive than initiating and managing a private foundation.

In terms of privacy, donor-advised funds offer an added shield. Unlike private foundations, DAFs are not obligated to disclose certain financial details, like tax returns.

Legacy giving involves leaving a bequest in your will or estate plan to a charitable organization or cause. This can be a way to make a significant contribution to a cause you care about and ensure that your legacy lives on. You can donate it in your name.

Legacy giving, despite being viewed as complex and accompanied by technical tax issues, can be an invaluable addition to your nonprofit's fundraising strategy.

The Importance of Legacy Giving

These planned gifts can take many forms, including monetary donations, real estate, or setting up a charitable annuity or trust.

Legacy giving benefits both donors and nonprofits. For nonprofits, legacy giving can create a stable and sustainable revenue source, build an endowment, deepen connections with donors, and diversify the types of assets received from donors.

Understanding Legacy Donations

If your organization plans to incorporate a program for legacy giving, grasping the various legacy donation options is pivotal. Here's a rundown of several types you might consider:

Estate Gifts: These represent the most frequently used and simplest variety of legacy giving. Estate gifts enable benefactors to determine what they'd like to donate to your organization within their will, for example, a specified sum of money, art pieces, equities, or a portion of their estate's overall worth.

Life Assurance: Contributors have the option to list your nonprofit as their life assurance policy's recipient or donate the accumulated value of the policy if it's no longer necessary for them.

Deferred Pension Plans: Those with tax-deferred pension plans can select your nonprofit as the beneficiary or specify a proportion of the benefits to be directed towards your organization.

Charitable Annuities: Bigger nonprofits can establish charitable annuities for their benefactors. Here, the donor offers a sizable donation while they are still alive, and the nonprofit reciprocates by providing a fixed income for the duration of the donor's life. Upon the donor's death, the remaining funds are directed to the nonprofit.

Life Estate Reserved: Donors can bestow a property to a nonprofit but maintain the right to inhabit it for their lifetime. Following the donor's death, the nonprofit can decide whether to retain or sell the property.

Implementing a Legacy Giving Program

To successfully incorporate legacy giving into your nonprofit's fundraising strategy, follow these steps:

1. Educate your organization's leadership and staff about the importance and benefits of legacy giving. Ensure that everyone understands the various types of legacy gifts and their potential impact on your nonprofit's long-term financial stability.

2. Develop a marketing strategy to promote your legacy giving program. Use your organization's website, newsletters, social media platforms, and other communication channels to inform donors and supporters about the various legacy giving options available.
3. Offer resources and guidance to help donors navigate the process of making a legacy gift. Provide information about the different types of legacy giving, the tax implications of each, and the steps involved in setting up a planned gift.
4. Seek professional advice from legal and financial experts, when necessary, especially when dealing with complex giving arrangements such as charitable gift annuities or retained life estates.
5. Regularly review and update your legacy giving program to ensure its effectiveness and relevance. Track the results of your marketing efforts, monitor the performance of your endowment, and adjust as needed.

VOLUNTEER WORK

You can make a positive impact on your community by volunteering your time and expertise to local organizations, such as schools, churches, or non-profits. This can include serving on boards or committees, mentoring young people, or providing pro bono services.

Volunteering offers a unique opportunity to help others, contribute to meaningful projects, and connect with communities around the world. By dedicating your time and skills, you can make a significant impact on the lives of others while enriching your own personal and professional growth.

Find a specialized volunteer work site

Start by browsing dedicated websites and platforms that connect volunteers with hosts in need of assistance. Websites like Worldpackers.com offer a wide range of opportunities, including social projects, NGOs, communities, ecovillages, and more. By signing up with such platforms, you can access an extensive database of volunteering opportunities worldwide.

Decide the period of the trip and time working

Consider how much time you can dedicate to volunteering and traveling. Establish a clear understanding of the work hours and days expected from you and ensure that you have enough free time to explore and relax. Whether you're volunteering at a temporary event or working on a long-term project, it's important to strike a balance between work and leisure.

Example: A volunteer might choose to work at an environmental conservation project in Costa Rica for two months, dedicating 20 hours per week to the cause while having ample time to explore the country's natural beauty.

Think about the skills you want to contribute

Take some time to list the intellectual, physical, and general skills you possess. Your unique skill set may include language abilities, musical talents, cooking expertise, or technical know-how. By identifying your strengths, you can find a volunteer opportunity that best aligns with your skills and interests.

Choose a volunteer cause for your trip

Reflect on the type of cause(s) you want to support. This could involve humanitarian efforts, environmental conservation, or community-based initiatives. If you're unsure, consider volunteering locally first to gain experience before venturing abroad.

Example: A volunteer with a background in healthcare might decide to join a medical mission in a developing country to help provide basic healthcare services to underserved communities.

Contact social projects that interest you

Once you've identified potential projects, reach out to the hosts, and discuss your expectations and any questions you may have. Be transparent about your needs, and inquire about accommodations, food, work expectations, and any additional benefits. Establishing clear communication from the outset will help avoid misunderstandings and ensure a smoother volunteering experience.

Create a budget

Consider the costs associated with your volunteer trip, including transportation, travel insurance, food, souvenirs, and emergency funds. Many volunteer opportunities provide accommodation and meals, which can significantly reduce your expenses. By carefully budgeting, you can determine when your volunteer adventure can become a reality.

Example: A volunteer planning a six-week trip to teach English in Southeast Asia might budget for airfare, visa fees, vaccinations, travel insurance, and additional spending money for excursions and souvenirs.

Start planning the trip

With all the necessary information in hand, it's time to plan your volunteer adventure. Purchase plane tickets in advance, confirm arrival details with your host, and gather any essential items you may need. Most importantly, prepare your mind and heart for the transformative experience ahead.

Example: A volunteer heading to a remote community in Africa might need to purchase a mosquito net, appropriate clothing, and any required vaccinations before departure.

ARTISTIC OR CULTURAL CONTRIBUTIONS

You can leave a lasting impact on the world through your artistic or cultural contributions. This can include creating art, writing books or music, or documenting your family's history and traditions.

The world is a tapestry of diverse cultures, languages, and artistic expressions. As individuals, we each possess unique talents, experiences, and perspectives that can leave a lasting impact on the world.

Creating Art

Whether you are a painter, sculptor, photographer, or digital artist, your creations can leave a lasting impact on those who encounter them. By sharing your art with the world, you contribute to a global dialogue that transcends language and cultural barriers.

Example: Frida Kahlo, a Mexican painter, used her artwork to express her emotions, experiences, and cultural heritage. Her paintings continue to inspire and influence artists worldwide.

Writing Books or Music

Authors and composers have the power to transport their audiences to new worlds, challenge existing norms, and inspire future generations. Whether you write fiction, non-fiction, poetry, or music, your creative works can resonate with readers and listeners across the globe, sparking new ideas and fostering a sense of shared humanity.

Example: The novel "To Kill a Mockingbird" by Harper Lee has become a classic in American literature, shedding light on racial injustice and moral growth. Its impact continues to be felt by readers worldwide.

Documenting Family History and Traditions

Every family has a unique story to tell, shaped by generations of ancestors and cultural traditions. By documenting your family's history and customs, you not only preserve your heritage for future generations but also contribute to a broader understanding of the diverse tapestry of human civilization.

Example: Alex Haley's "Roots: The Saga of an American Family" traces the author's ancestry back to 18th-century Africa and provides a compelling account of the African American experience over several generations.

Participating in Cultural Events and Festivals

Partaking in cultural events and festivals allows you to share your heritage with others while immersing yourself in the customs and traditions of different communities. By participating in such gatherings, you foster cross-cultural understanding and appreciation, ultimately contributing to a more harmonious and interconnected world.

Example: Diwali, the Festival of Lights, is celebrated by millions of people worldwide. The exchange of cultural practices and traditions during this time contributes to a deeper understanding of the diverse beliefs and customs that shape our world.

Sharing Your Skills and Knowledge

Sharing your artistic or cultural skills and knowledge with others is another way to leave a lasting impact. This could involve teaching a dance class, leading a writing workshop, or organizing a cultural exchange program. By passing on your expertise, you empower others to express themselves creatively and engage with their own cultural heritage.

Example: Yo-Yo Ma, a renowned cellist, founded the Silk Road Ensemble to promote cross-cultural collaboration and understanding through music. This initiative has inspired countless musicians and audiences across the globe.

Donating to Community Structures

Donating to community structures like park benches, play parks, water fountains, dog parks, exercise areas, or community center contributions.

Donor-advised funds (DAFs) allow individuals, families, and businesses to make tax-deductible charitable contributions to a sponsoring organization, such as a community foundation, which then manages the funds. Donors can recommend grants from the fund to qualified nonprofit organizations over time, thus providing a more strategic and flexible approach to their philanthropy.

DAFs have seen significant growth in recent years, with the number of DAF accounts surpassing 873,000 in 2020. Critics argue that DAFs can lead to a lack of transparency and accountability, as donors can remain anonymous, and funds can sit in DAFs indefinitely without being granted to nonprofits. However, proponents of DAFs highlight their accessibility, simplicity, and convenience as reasons for their popularity among donors.

Impact Investing

While impact investing is still a relatively small portion of overall philanthropic activity, it has the potential to play a significant role in addressing global challenges.

Family Philanthropy

Family philanthropy is a long-standing tradition in which families come together to pool their resources and expertise to support causes that align with their shared values. Family philanthropy can help foster a culture of giving and civic engagement within families and pass down values of generosity and community involvement to future generations.

One notable trend in family philanthropy is the increasing involvement of younger generations in decision-making processes.

The landscape of strategic giving and civic engagement is vast and varied, with numerous ways for individuals and organizations to make a lasting impact. As society continues to face complex challenges, philanthropy and civic engagement will play a crucial role in driving positive change and fostering a thriving democracy.

Ways to Get Involved/What You Can Do

1. Reflect on your values and passions: Consider what causes are most important to you and how you want to make a difference in the world.
2. Research organizations and causes: Investigate nonprofits and initiatives that align with your values and interests, and explore different giving vehicles, such as DAFs or impact investing.
3. Volunteer your time and expertise: Engage in your community by volunteering with local organizations or joining a board of directors.

4. Advocate for policy changes: Stay informed about policies that impact philanthropy and nonprofit organizations and use your voice to support or oppose legislation when necessary.
5. Involve your family and friends: Share your giving experiences and encourage others to join you in supporting causes that matter to you.

Additional Resources

1. Giving USA: Provides comprehensive data and insights on charitable giving trends in the United States.
2. The Women's Philanthropy Institute: Conducts research on gender differences in giving and offers resources to help women maximize their philanthropic impact.
3. The Urban Institute's Center on Nonprofits and Philanthropy

SOCIAL MEDIA AND ONLINE PRESENCE

You can also impact the world through your online presence, by sharing your ideas and experiences with a wider audience. You can use social media to share your views on important issues or create a blog or website to promote causes you care about.

Tips to Building a Better Social Media Presence

1. Set SMART goals: This will help you avoid aimless posting and focus on what truly matters for your brand.
2. Identify your audience: Understand who you want to reach with your social media efforts. This will inform which platforms

you should be active on, the type of content you should create, and the tone of your messaging.

3. Be human: Let your brand's personality shine through social media. This means engaging with your audience in a genuine and personal manner, sharing behind-the-scenes content, and showcasing the people behind your brand.

4. Seek relationships, not just followers: Focus on building meaningful connections with your audience rather than simply trying to amass many followers. Engage in conversations, answer questions, and foster a sense of community.

5. Create an editorial calendar: This will help you stay organized, maximize the reach of your content, and ensure you are sharing a diverse range of posts.

6. Automate the right way: Use automation tools to help with content scheduling and curation but avoid using them for customer care or interactions with your audience, as this can come across as insincere.

7. Focus on helping over selling: Provide value to your audience by offering solutions to their problems, rather than constantly pushing your products or services. This can help establish your brand as an authority and foster trust among your followers.

8. Optimize your accounts for engagement: Ensure your social media profiles are fully filled out and include relevant keywords, imagery, and information. This can help attract more followers and make it easier for people to find and engage with your content.

9. When in doubt, get visual: Embrace the power of photos and videos in your social media strategy. Visual content consistently performs well across platforms, so incorporate it into your posts whenever possible.

10. Make your presence known: Promote your social media accounts across your website, email signatures, and other marketing channels to encourage people to connect with your brand on social platforms.

11. Stay active: Maintain a regular presence on your chosen social media platforms by posting fresh content and engaging with your audience consistently.

12. Piggyback on what's trending: Join in on relevant trending topics or hashtags to showcase your brand's personality and stay current with popular culture. Be mindful not to engage in controversial topics that could alienate your audience.

13. Don't be afraid to pay: Invest in social media advertising or influencer partnerships to amplify your reach and achieve specific goals. Both strategies can deliver impressive ROI when executed well.

14. Use tools to monitor your activity: Leverage analytics tools to track the performance of your social media efforts, identify trends, and make data-driven decisions. This will help you refine your strategy and maximize the impact of your social media presence.

15. Continuously learn and adapt: social media is an ever-changing landscape. Stay informed about platform updates, new trends, and best practices to ensure your social media strategy

remains effective and relevant. Be open to adjusting your approach as needed to keep up with the evolving digital world.

CHAPTER SUMMARY

The Importance of a Coherent Estate Plan

A comprehensive estate plan, encompassing all decisions and choices, is pivotal for streamlined estate planning. A well-devised estate plan does not only promise peace of mind for you and your family but also mitigates potential legal complexities, tax burdens, and stress during a time of emotional distress.

Compiling Legal Documents

Every document has a specific role, and it is imperative to ensure their coherence and alignment. For instance, should you set up a trust for managing your assets, it's crucial to revise your will and beneficiary specifications on insurance policies or retirement accounts to mirror this modification.

Integrating Financial and Tax Planning

A robust estate plan should factor in the financial and tax ramifications of your decisions. This often entails collaborating with financial advisors, accountants, and lawyers to devise a comprehensive strategy that curtails tax liabilities and augments your estate's value. Strategies such as lifetime gifting, philanthropy, or the establishment of an Irrevocable Life Insurance Trust (ILIT) can help in reducing estate taxes and preserving your assets for subsequent generations.

Synchronizing Beneficiaries

A prevalent oversight in estate planning is neglecting to update beneficiary specifications on accounts like life insurance policies, retirement schemes, and bank accounts. Regular review of these designations is necessary to ensure alignment with your broader estate plan. For instance, if you've listed your spouse as your life insurance policy's primary beneficiary but later form a trust for your children's benefit, you should modify the beneficiary specification accordingly.

Including Business Succession Planning

For business owners, addressing business succession within the estate plan is essential. A carefully devised succession plan facilitates a smooth transition of management and ownership, mitigates potential familial conflicts, and safeguards the business's value. This could mean formulating a buy-sell agreement, instituting a family limited partnership, or setting up a trust to hold business interests.

Incorporating Digital Assets

With the digital age upon us, integrating your digital assets into your estate plan is of growing importance. This includes online accounts, social media handles, and digital files or documents housed on your personal computer or cloud. For smooth integration, share a detailed list of your digital assets, with corresponding usernames and passwords, with your executor or trustee. Also, offer explicit instructions about the management or distribution of these assets.

Engaging with Family and Professionals

Lastly, clear communication with your family members and professionals participating in your estate planning process is key for a well-integrated estate plan. It helps prevent miscommunication, reduces potential disputes, and ensures everyone involved is on the same wavelength regarding the execution of your estate plan. It's worth considering family meetings to discuss your plans and intentions and sharing relevant documents with your executor, trustee, and other professionals engaged in your estate planning process.

PART 3: LEGACY

CHAPTER SEVEN

SHIELDING & SHELTERING YOUR WEALTH

The legal right of a taxpayer to decrease the amount of what otherwise would be his taxes, or altogether to avoid them, by means which the law permits, cannot be doubted.

– George Sutherland, U.S. Supreme Court Justice

YOU CAN'T TAKE IT WITH YOU…

What is the single largest expense most people have in their golden years, in their retirement? Is it mortgage payments? Is it healthcare? No. Generally, from the income tax returns that we review and prepare, the single largest bill that you are going to pay in your later years, your hopefully golden years, is going to be the payment of income taxes on your income.

In most instances, the Internal Revenue Service and your State taxing authority collect more because most people don't know how to shield and shelter their income effectively. In our tax practice we have twenty three (23) time tested tax strategies to shield, shelter, and minimize tax liabilities of our clients. The top 5 are strategies most can use and depending on your portfolio there are likely two to three others the bulk of the tax paying public could use.

Retirement planning can be a daunting task, and the anxiety surrounding it is often fueled by common myths and misconceptions. Dispelling these myths can help you feel more confident in preparing for your golden years and eliminate unnecessary worry. Let's review some of the retirement planning myths you should avoid:

- Retirement means the end of work: Many people assume that retirement means they will never work again. While it's true that you may no longer be working full-time, you may still have part-time work or volunteer opportunities that keep you busy.
- You need to be wealthy to retire: Retirement planning is not only for the wealthy. With careful planning, anyone can save and invest for retirement. It's important to start saving early, even if it's just a small amount each month.
- Social Security is designed to be a supplement to your retirement savings, not a replacement for it. Depending solely on Social Security may not be enough to cover your expenses in retirement.
- You can't save enough for retirement: Saving for retirement is a long-term process, and it's never too late to start. Even if you start saving later in life, you can still make a significant impact on your retirement savings.

- You will be bored in retirement: Retirement can be a time to pursue hobbies, travel, and spend time with family and friends. It's an opportunity to explore new interests and experiences.
- You will spend less in retirement: While it's true that some expenses, such as work-related costs, may decrease in retirement, other expenses, such as healthcare, may increase. It's important to plan for both.
- You should wait until you're older to start saving for retirement: The earlier you start saving for retirement, the more time your money has to grow. Starting early will make a big difference in the amount of money you have when you retire.
- You can rely on your employer's retirement plan: It's important to have a diversified retirement plan that includes individual savings and investments.
- You can dip into your retirement savings without consequences: Withdrawing money from your retirement savings before retirement can result in penalties and taxes and can also reduce the amount of money you have available in retirement.
- Retirement planning is too complicated: While retirement planning can seem overwhelming, many resources are available to help you. Financial advisors, retirement calculators, and online resources can all be useful tools in planning for retirement.

Not long-ago Forbes magazine outlined three (3) key myths you should recognize and then take action to control your financial future and work towards creating a retirement plan that suits your needs and goals. Embrace the truth behind these misconceptions and start building a retirement strategy that brings you peace of mind and financial security.

Myth #1: Social Security will be phased out

While it's true that the Social Security trust fund faces challenges, it's unlikely that the program will disappear entirely. Politicians understand the importance of Social Security for millions of Americans and are likely to take steps to ensure its survival. Instead of worrying about the program's demise, focus on the fact that Social Security benefits will continue to play a role in your retirement planning.

Myth #2: Stock Market and Home Appreciation are Retirement Risks

Although the performance of the stock market and home values are important factors in your retirement planning, they aren't the biggest risks.

Myth #3: Saving for Retirement is unaffordable

Despite financial challenges faced by younger generations, such as student loans and economic instability, it's possible to begin saving for retirement. It's crucial to develop the habit of saving early, even if you start with a small amount. You can always increase your savings as your income grows. Additionally, everyone has access to traditional or Roth individual retirement accounts (IRAs), regardless of whether their employer offers a retirement plan.

How to Plan for Retirement

Retirement Planning: Key Steps and Strategies

As retirement looms on the horizon, it's vital to craft a strategy that guarantees a secure and comfortable post-work life. Below are some critical steps and strategies for effective retirement planning.

Evaluate Your Present Financial Status

Closely examine your existing financial circumstances, including your earnings, expenditures, assets, and debts. This provides a transparent understanding of your financial health and highlights areas needing attention as retirement approaches.

Craft a Detailed Retirement Budget

A well-thought-out retirement budget allows you to estimate potential retirement costs, including housing, healthcare, and daily living expenses. It's important to factor in inflation as costs are likely to rise over time. Also, consider any lifestyle modifications you foresee during retirement, such as pursuing new hobbies, traveling, or downsizing your residence.

Expand Your Income Streams

Dependence on Social Security benefits or a retirement plan might not provide enough for a comfortable retirement. Diversifying your income streams through various investment avenues, such as equities, bonds, mutual funds, real estate, and annuities, is advisable.

A diversified portfolio can provide a consistent income in retirement while mitigating risks.

Devise an Estate Plan

Estate planning is an integral part of retirement planning. It ensures that your wealth, assets, and income are distributed according to your desires, minimizing the chances of family conflicts. Engage with a legal professional to draft a will, establish a trust, appoint beneficiaries, and prepare any essential legal documents like powers of attorney and healthcare directives. You can also opt for a do-it-yourself approach or employ a hybrid strategy.

In essence, the process of estate planning brings two fundamental options to the forefront: one, shoulder the entire process by yourself, spending a significant amount of time and energy on extensive research; or two, engage the services of an attorney, placing your hopes in the assumption that they are the right professional for your unique needs.

However, an important distinction to bear in mind is that attorneys, by the nature of their profession, focus predominantly on the preparation of legal documents. While this is undoubtedly a crucial aspect of estate planning, it does not cover all bases. They are not necessarily equipped, nor are they expected to assist with every facet of the process.

Estate planning is a multi-layered journey with several integral components. Beyond the drafting of legal documents, the process encompasses tax implications and comprehensive planning. These aspects are best handled by professionals who specialize in those fields — a CPA or an accountant for tax considerations and a financial planner for the planning aspect.

The unfortunate reality, however, is that these professionals, each valuable, do not typically cross into each other's lanes. Attorneys stick to legal documents, financial planners to planning, and CPAs to tax considerations, none are willing, and often legally unable, to give advice beyond their respective expertise.

Our business seeks to bridge this gap. We position ourselves at the heart of these complexities, coordinating and synchronizing the various components of estate planning. The objective is not to replace these professionals, but to ensure the whole process is seamlessly integrated.

The statement, "worked with an attorney to create a will," does indeed indicate progress, but it is essential to remember that it does not represent completion. It is merely one piece of the puzzle. The other components — tax implications, financial planning — optimization, i.e. having them work together, ideally is the rule, not the exception.

The takeaway here is clear: hiring an attorney to draft a will is indeed an important step, but it is not the panacea for all your estate planning needs. You still need to grapple with tax liabilities, tax planning which includes maximum use of tax reduction strategies, and frankly a process to weave all these elements together into a comprehensive estate plan.

Plan for potential tax implications

Retirement can bring various tax implications, such as required minimum distributions from retirement accounts, Social Security taxation, and estate taxes. Work with a financial advisor to develop a tax-efficient retirement plan that minimizes your tax liabilities and maximizes your retirement income.

Stay informed about changes in laws and regulations.

Laws and regulations related to estate planning, tax policies, and retirement accounts are subject to change.

Review and adjust your plan regularly.

Retirement planning is an ongoing process that requires regular review and adjustment. As your financial situation, goals, and needs change, be prepared to revise your retirement plan accordingly. This will help ensure that your plan remains aligned with your objectives and circumstances throughout your retirement years.

CREATE A RETIREMENT SAVINGS PLAN

Achieving a comfortable retirement requires a well-thought-out investment strategy that aligns with your long-term goals. Evaluating your investment portfolio is an essential step in ensuring your financial well-being during your golden years. Here are some key aspects to consider when assessing your investment portfolio:

1. Diversification

A diversified investment portfolio helps spread risk and enhances the potential for returns. By allocating your assets across different investment types (stocks, bonds, real estate, etc.) and sectors, you can minimize the impact of market fluctuations on your overall portfolio. Rebalance your investments periodically to maintain the desired level of diversification and adjust your holdings as you move closer to retirement.

2. Risk Tolerance

As you progress through different stages of life, your risk tolerance may change. While a more aggressive investment approach might have been suitable in your earlier years, it's essential to reassess your risk tolerance as you approach retirement. This may involve shifting your investments towards more conservative, income-generating assets to protect your retirement nest egg.

3. Investment Time Horizon

Your investment horizon, or the time you have before needing to access your retirement funds, will affect your investment strategy.

4. Financial Goals

Reevaluate your financial goals periodically to ensure your investment portfolio is aligned with your retirement objectives. This may involve increasing your savings rate, adjusting your investment mix, or revisiting your retirement income needs. Stay adaptable and be prepared to modify your investment strategy to accommodate any changes in your personal or financial circumstances.

EVALUATE YOUR INVESTMENT PORTFOLIO

A healthy investment portfolio is vital to your financial stability and plays a crucial role in your overall estate planning strategy. In this chapter, we will delve into the importance of evaluating your investment portfolio and how to make informed decisions for your financial future.

1. The Importance of a Well-Diversified Portfolio

Diversification helps you balance risk and reward, ensuring that your investment strategy supports your long-term financial goals and estate planning objectives.

2. Regularly Review Your Investment Portfolio

Just as your life and financial goals change over time, so should your investment strategy. This allows you to make any necessary adjustments to your investment mix and ensure that your assets continue to work for you as you approach retirement.

3. Aligning Your Portfolio with Your Retirement Goals

Your investment portfolio should be designed to support your retirement goals and lifestyle preferences. Consider factors such as your desired retirement age, expected living expenses, and any additional income sources, such as Social Security or a pension.

4. Seeking Professional Guidance

A knowledgeable advisor can help you assess your risk tolerance, set realistic investment goals, and create a diversified portfolio that supports your long-term objectives.

Manage Debt

Dealing with debt can feel like an uphill battle, but managing it effectively is crucial for your financial health and peace of mind. To help you tackle your debt and work towards financial freedom, let's explore seven steps you can take to manage and reduce your debt more effectively.

Assess your debts

Begin by listing all your outstanding debts, including the interest rate for each. This will help you identify which debts are causing the most financial strain and should be prioritized for repayment.

Review your credit report

This will ensure you haven't overlooked any debts and allow you to verify there aren't any unrecognized accounts. Check with your bank or credit card company to see if they can provide your credit score at no cost.

Consider consolidation

If you have multiple high-interest loans, explore the possibility of consolidating them. A low-interest personal loan could help pay off high-interest credit card balances. Be cautious when consolidating or refinancing student loans, as this may impact your eligibility for federal loan forgiveness programs.

Evaluate your spending habits

Take an honest look at your monthly spending. Identify expenses that can be reduced or eliminated to prevent further debt accumulation.

Calculate your required payments

After consolidating your debts, determine your required monthly payments by noting the minimum amounts and including the total in your budget. If the total amount exceeds your budget, contact your lenders to discuss alternative payment terms.

Allocate extra funds towards debt repayment

With your required monthly payments in mind, determine how much additional money from your budget can be devoted to debt reduction.

Choose a debt-reduction strategy

Decide how to tackle your debt. The former can save more money in the long run, while the latter can provide a sense of progress and motivation. Whichever approach you choose, stick to your plan and stay focused on your goal of debt reduction.

Taking control of your debt is an essential step towards achieving peace of mind and ensuring your estate is well-managed.

A Must Do - Healthcare expenses

Healthcare expenses can be a significant concern for many, especially as costs tend to increase with age. To ensure a secure and comfortable lifestyle, it's essential to plan for these expenses early on. This section will help you navigate the various aspects of healthcare costs in retirement and provide strategies for managing them effectively.

Develop a lifestyle income plan:

A well-crafted lifestyle income planning strategy can help you achieve this goal. Here are eight steps to help you develop a retirement income plan that suits your needs and objectives. A financial advisor can also provide valuable guidance and advice tailored to your unique situation.

Develop a Solid Lifestyle Withdrawal Strategy

There are time-tested withdrawal strategies, such as the 4% rule, dynamic withdrawal strategy, or the bucket method. Each approach has pros and cons, and you should select the one that best aligns with your financial goals and risk tolerance.

Create a Tax Strategy on Lifestyle Plan Withdrawals

Minimize taxes on retirement plan withdrawals by strategically tapping into different accounts, like taxable investments, tax-deferred accounts (e.g., IRAs), and Roth IRAs, in a specific order to optimize tax efficiency.

Consider Rolling Over Your Savings to a Roth IRA

Roth IRAs offer tax-free withdrawals after age 59.5 (with a five-year account holding period) and no required minimum distributions, making them a valuable tool in your lifestyle income strategy.

Plan for a Long Retirement

Develop a retirement income plan that extends beyond your life expectancy to ensure you don't outlive your savings. Early and consistent planning is key to achieving a comfortable and secure retirement.

Stick to the Right Asset Allocation

Maintain an appropriate asset allocation that reflects your risk tolerance and financial goals, even during retirement. Periodically review and rebalance your portfolio to ensure it remains aligned with your objectives. A financial advisor can help you navigate this process and adjust as needed.

One of the most critical aspects of planning for your retirement is to review and adjust your plan regularly. Life is full of unexpected twists and turns, and your financial situation and goals may evolve over time.

A lifestyle income plan is a valuable tool in this process. It serves as a year-by-year timeline, showing where your lifestyle income will come from throughout your golden years. Creating a lifestyle income plan is similar to creating a budget, but it is designed to predict your spending needs over an extended period. Your retirement income may come from various sources, including Social Security, pensions, annuities, and part-time work. It's crucial to account for the full picture when planning for your retirement.

Remember that many financial factors can change over time, such as tax liability, inflation, and investment returns. By knowing how much income you'll have over time, you can better prepare for both planned spending and unforeseen expenses.

A simple DIY lifestyle income plan is to start by making a template with one row for each calendar year, alongside your respective age and, if applicable, your spouse's age. Extend this projection through your life expectancy. Then, list fixed sources of retirement income, such as Social Security, pensions, and annuities. Don't forget to include any part-time work or other income sources, such as rental income or alimony.

Next, estimate your total annual living expenses and add them to your plan. This should include items such as mortgage payments, taxes, and other regular expenses. Be aware that tax rates will vary depending on your total income and deductions, so it's essential to do tax planning each year to project this accurately.

Once you've listed all your income and expenses, calculate the gap between the two. This will help you determine whether you need to withdraw from savings or investments to maintain your desired retirement lifestyle, or if you have a surplus that can be added to savings or used for additional spending.

It's important to remember that this lifestyle income plan does not account for inflation or investment returns, but it serves as a starting point for outlining your retirement income sources. You can use this plan to create a customized investment strategy based on your projected withdrawals and financial needs.

Review and adjust your plan regularly!

TOP RETIREMENT MISTAKES

- Failing to start saving early: Often people delay saving for retirement, citing current needs as a rationale, believing they have time to catch up later. But the earlier you start, the more time your money has to grow, thanks to the power of compound interest. Start saving for retirement as soon as possible, even if it's a small amount.
- Not saving enough: Another common mistake is not saving enough for retirement. A general rule of thumb is to save at least 10% of your income each year for retirement. Those really motivated perhaps to retire even early will want to save at least 20%. If you start saving late, you will likely need to save more.
- Not diversifying your investments: Diversification is critical to managing risk in your retirement portfolio. Don't put all your eggs in one basket. Invest in a mix of stocks, bonds, and other assets that align with your retirement goals and risk tolerance.

- Withdrawing from retirement accounts early: Withdrawing from your retirement accounts before age 59 ½ can trigger penalties and taxes, which can reduce the amount of money you have available for retirement. Try to avoid withdrawing from your retirement accounts until you reach retirement age.
- Underestimating healthcare costs: Healthcare costs can be a significant expense in retirement. Consider buying long-term care insurance and plan for any medical expenses in your retirement budget.
- Failing to update your retirement plan: Life changes can impact your retirement plan, such as job loss, marriage, divorce, or a death in the family. Update your retirement plan regularly to ensure it is still aligned with your goals and financial situation.
- Relying too heavily on Social Security: Social Security was originally designed and is still considered to be a supplement to your retirement savings, not a replacement for it. Plan for additional income sources in retirement, such as a pension or personal savings
- Not seeking professional advice: Retirement planning is complex, and seeking professional advice can help you avoid mistakes and optimize your retirement plan.

WHAT'S MY NUMBER?

How Much Money Do I Need to Retire Comfortably?

Frankly, there are many variables to consider, such as your desired lifestyle, financial goals, and life expectancy. To help you make sense of these factors, we have included this section to help you calculate how much you'll need per month to live your intended retirement lifestyle.

Instead, consider using a combination of annuities and Social Security Income to provide a guaranteed monthly income stream that won't run out. This can help ensure that you have enough savings to retire comfortably at your desired age.

How Much Should I Save for Retirement Each Year?

I advise saving at least 20% of your gross income towards retirement each year. This percentage may need to be adjusted based on your circumstances, such as your desired retirement lifestyle, expected retirement age, life expectancy, and current savings.

Calculate How Much Income You Need For Retirement

I advise that we look first at your guaranteed income, then the variable income, then determine how much lifestyle you can afford to live. To determine guaranteed income first look at any pension income, then social security, then annuities. You may need to delay retirement if your guaranteed income sources don't cover your monthly expenses.

Use the following link to access over 150 calculators to help you estimate retirement, healthcare costs, estate planning, taxation, investment, etc. https://www.owatax.com/Resources/ Be sure to scroll down the long list to find the right resource for your needs.

By the way, one of the special gems on our main page is the "Tax Bill in Retirement" button. 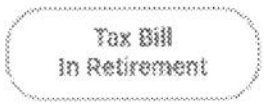

Here, if you enter your current savings, age, and desired retirement age, my office will send you a personalized report data based on your situation. Take advantage.

Why Use Annuities?

Annuities are contractual plans that provide a fixed income for life on a guaranteed basis. They offer a lifetime income stream similar to a pension plan, making them a reliable source of retirement income.

Retirement Savings Account Comparison

Compare annuities with other retirement savings accounts like 401(k)s, IRAs, and Roth IRAs to understand the differences in withdrawal percentages, income increase potential, annual fees, and taxation.

How Much Do I Need To Retire At Various Ages?

To retire at different ages with a specific annual income, you'll need varying amounts of retirement savings. The tables provided outline the deposit amounts needed for different retirement ages to receive a certain annual income through an annuity.

To determine how much you will need each month in retirement, estimate your expected monthly expenses in the categories below. Then total the amounts to see your estimated monthly retirement budget.

Housing (mortgage/rent, prop. taxes, insurance): $___________

Utilities (electric, water, cable): $__________

Food (groceries and dining out): $__________

Transportation (car payment, gas, public transit): $__________

Medical (insurance premiums, out-of-pocket costs): $________

Debt payments (loans, credit cards): $__________

Entertainment (travel, hobbies, subscriptions): $__________

Discretionary (gifts, donations, misc.): $__________

Monthly total: $__________

To generate annual income from this monthly budget in retirement, multiply the total by 12. For example, if your monthly total is $3,000, your annual retirement income needed would be $3,000 x 12 = $36,000.

As we progress through life, our needs and priorities inevitably change. It's crucial to consider the potential increased costs and evolving requirements as you age. Here is the importance of making provisions for yourself and discussing various ways to prepare for the unexpected. Here's a high-level checklist:

1. Emergency fund: By definition, unexpected expenses occur unexpectantly and having an emergency fund will help you manage these costs without depleting your retirement savings. Target setting aside three to six months' worth of living expenses in an easily accessible account to cover unforeseen expenses, such as medical emergencies, home repairs, or temporary loss of income.

2. Estate planning updates: As your circumstances change, it's essential to review and update your estate plan regularly. This may include updating your will, adjusting your beneficiaries, or revising your trusts. By keeping your estate plan current, you can ensure that your wealth, assets and incomes are distributed according to your wishes and minimize the potential for family disputes.
3. Diversify your investments: With the potential for increased costs and needs as you age, it's crucial to have a diversified investment portfolio that can provide growth and income in your retirement years. Work with a financial advisor to create a well-balanced portfolio that aligns with your risk tolerance and financial goals.
4. Consider downsizing: As you age, your housing needs may change. Downsizing to a smaller home or moving to a retirement community can reduce your expenses, simplify your lifestyle, and free up funds for other priorities.

Chapter Summary

The chapter emphasized Sheltering and Shielding your wealth from threats that minimize it, with the biggest threat being taxation. The best course of action is to have a written plan developed that is customized to your specific goals, needs, and wants. With the plan in hand it is easier to decide on the best strategies to lower taxes and create a stable, lifelong income. There are several key choices and decisions to be made in consultation with your financial advisors. In the next chapter, we'll review dozens of estate planning strategies and provide a checklist to get started on implementation.

CHAPTER EIGHT

STEP-BY-STEP ESTATE PLANNING STRATEGIES

What we need to do is always lean into the future; when the world changes around you and when it changes against you - what used to be a tail wind is now a head wind - you have to lean into that and figure out what to do because complaining isn't a strategy.

– Jeff Bezos

YOU CAN DO THIS

As you begin the estate planning process, it's essential to define your strategic objectives, which will serve as the foundation for your overall plan.

Identifying Your Strategic Objectives

Before you can create a successful estate plan, you must first identify your strategic objectives. These goals will vary depending on your personal situation, financial status, and desires for your family and legacy. Some common strategic objectives in estate planning might include:

- Ensuring financial security for your spouse or partner.
- Providing for your children's education and future needs.
- Minimizing taxes and expenses associated with your estate.

- Supporting charitable causes that are important to you.
- Preserving your family's wealth for future generations.
- Avoiding family conflicts over inheritance.

Writing Out Your Strategic Objectives

Once you have identified your strategic objectives, it's essential to write them out clearly and concisely. This will help you communicate your goals effectively to your family, attorney, and financial advisors. When writing out your strategic objectives, be specific and actionable. For example, instead of writing "provide for my children," consider writing "establish a trust to fund my children's education and support them until they reach age 25."

Aligning Your Estate Plan with Your Strategic Objectives

With your strategic objectives defined and written out, you can begin developing an estate plan that aligns with your goals. As you create your estate plan, continually refer to your strategic objectives to ensure that each element supports your overall goals.

For example, if one of your strategic objectives is to minimize estate taxes, you might work with your attorney to establish a charitable remainder trust (CRT).

Reviewing and Updating Your Strategic Objectives

As your life circumstances change, your strategic objectives may need to be updated to reflect your current goals and priorities. Regularly reviewing and updating your strategic objectives will ensure that your estate plan remains aligned with your desires, even as your family and financial situations evolve.

For instance, if you initially set a strategic objective to provide for your children's education but later discover that they have received full scholarships, you may decide to redirect the trust funds to support their future endeavors, such as starting a business or buying a home.

Your estate planning objectives, which include various aspects of your estate, form the basis of your estate planning strategy. These objectives are crucial when it comes to organizing your estate in a way that ensures your legacy is managed and distributed according to your wishes. In this comprehensive guide, we'll go through the step-by-step process of creating estate planning strategies, with examples provided for clarity.

Step-by-Step Guide to Estate Planning Strategies

Identify goals based on your specific needs, not on general guidelines.

Your estate planning goals should be tailored to your unique circumstances and desires, rather than simply following a standard template. For instance, if you have a blended family, your objectives may involve ensuring that both your current spouse and children from a previous marriage are taken care of. Alternatively, if you own a family business, you may prioritize succession planning and business continuity.

Be sure to base your estate planning objectives on your specific needs and situation.

Address all key aspects of estate planning when setting objectives.

Estate planning covers various areas, including financial management, asset distribution, tax planning, healthcare directives, and guardianship decisions. When setting your objectives, ensure that they cover each of these aspects comprehensively.

Adopt the "Goal + Timeframe + Action to drive your thinking.

A well-defined estate planning objective should include a goal, a timeframe, and action. This format ensures that your goals become reality.

For example, the goal could be to "Cut estate tax liability by establishing a trust within the next six months."

Develop clear and concise goal statements.

A goal statement should provide additional context and explanation for your estate planning objectives. These statements, usually no more than 2-3 sentences, clarify the intent and meaning of each objective.

For example, if the goal is "Appoint a legal guardian for minor children," the goal statement might be:

"We will designate a trusted family member or friend as the legal guardian of our minor children to ensure their wellbeing and upbringing align with our values and expectations."

Follow these guidelines when setting estate planning objectives.

Limit your objectives to a manageable number, focusing on the most critical aspects of your estate.

Ensure your objectives are coherent and complement each other.

Clearly define your goals with specific actions and targets.

Avoid including short-term tasks or projects as goals.

Common Estate Planning Goals

- Financial Management
- Maintain financial stability for surviving spouses.
- Preserve family wealth for future generations.
- Ensure sufficient liquidity to cover estate expenses.
- Asset Distribution
- Distribute assets fairly among heirs.
- Transfer specific assets to designated beneficiaries.
- Establish trusts to manage assets for minor children.
- Tax Planning
- Minimize estate and inheritance taxes.
- Implement tax-efficient gifting strategies.
- Healthcare Directives
- Appoint a healthcare proxy to make medical decisions.
- Establish advance directives for end-of-life care.
- Set up a trust to provide financial support for dependents.

Case Example: The Franklin Family Estate

In this example, the Franklin's family's estate planning objectives focus on providing for their four children, minimizing estate taxes, and ensuring a smooth transition of their family business to the next generation.

Case Example: The Johnson Family Estate

The Johnson family's estate planning objectives emphasize the importance of charitable giving, providing for their disabled child, and distributing their assets in a fair and equitable manner among their remaining children.

Getting Started…

The best way to begin the process of setting your estate planning objectives is to ask yourself key questions, for example:

Asset Distribution: How do you envision distributing your assets among your heirs?

Tax Planning: What strategies can you implement to minimize estate taxes and other liabilities?

Healthcare Directives: What are your preferences for medical care and decision-making in case of incapacity?

Guardianship Decisions: Who do you trust to care for your minor children or dependents with special needs?

STEP-BY-STEP ESTATE PLANNING STRATEGIES

Focus on Wealth Management

Proper wealth management is essential to preserve your assets and grow your estate. Implementing a sound investment strategy can ensure your wealth is optimized and protected against market volatility.

Protect Assets and Reduce Risk

Protecting your assets from potential creditors or lawsuits is a vital part of estate planning. Establishing trusts, using insurance products, and adopting appropriate business structures can help shield your assets from unexpected liabilities.

Minimize Tax Burdens

Reducing the impact of taxes on your estate is crucial for preserving your wealth for your beneficiaries. Utilizing strategies such as gifting assets during your lifetime to minimize your estate's tax liabilities. Consulting with a tax professional or estate planning attorney is highly recommended to ensure you comply with tax laws while maximizing tax-saving opportunities.

Business Owners Should Have Succession Planning

If you own a business, succession planning should be a part of your estate plan. This involves determining how ownership and management of the business will be transferred upon your death or retirement, ensuring a smooth transition and minimizing disruption to the business.

Have Trusted Key Players Carry Out Your Estate Plan

Your estate plan should include trusted individuals or professionals to carry out your wishes, such as an executor, trustee, or attorney-in-fact. These individuals will be responsible for managing your assets, making decisions on your behalf, and ensuring your estate plan is implemented according to your wishes.

Structured Investments to Pay Out in Your Old Age

Estate planning should also consider strategies for generating income during your retirement years. Structured investments, such as annuities or dividend-paying stocks, can provide a steady stream of income to help cover living expenses and healthcare costs.

Topic for focus

We typically have a topic for focus and action when we meet with clients. Here's a partial list for you to broach with your advisor(s):

Wealth Management

- Diversify your investment portfolio
- Rebalance your assets regularly
- Implement tax-efficient investment strategies

Asset Protection

- Establish trusts for asset protection
- Use life insurance products to secure your wealth
- Set up appropriate business structures to limit liability

Tax Minimization

- Make annual tax-free gifts to beneficiaries
- Utilize the estate tax exemption
- Fill the bucket/bracket to lower Medicare taxes

Getting Started By Using This Action Checklist

Use this checklist to kickstart your estate planning goals/strategies:

[ ] Grow and manage wealth for the long run

[ ] Protect assets and reduce risks

[ ] Minimize taxes on your estate

[ ] Plan for business succession

[ ] Have trusted executors implement your plan

[ ] Generate income in retirement

[ ] Strategy 1: Develop financial plans and investment trusts to reach high returns and generational wealth

[ ] Strategy 2: Implement asset protection structures and insurance to avoid threat risks and pass safe wealth

[ ] Strategy 3: Plan testamentary trusts, charitable trusts and gifting to cut estate, capital gains and beneficiary tax

[ ] Strategy 4: Create business succession roadmap to transfer ownership, shareholdings and roles without disputes to retain value

[ ] Strategy 5: Appoint executors in family and advisory teams to navigate wills and complex strategic issues implementing your Estate Wishes

[ ] Strategy 6: Develop annuities, account pensions and allocated income streams for financial security and stability in your retirement plan

Notes:

____

____

____

____

CHAPTER SUMMARY

If you are not careful, the critical nature of a good estate plan can be overwhelming in the beginning. We advise our clients to develop a plan and identify the top three issues to address first, focusing on only one at a time. Then, act and implement it. This chapter provides a number of strategies for review and consideration. Develop your plan, focus on one, and take action. If we can help, just call or email us.

CHAPTER NINE

THE SINGLE LIFE

Charity begins at home but should not end there.

- Thomas Fuller

Life happens and you may find yourself in a place where you are living alone or have few or no direct beneficiaries. In such cases, estate planning takes on a different dimension, with specific considerations and challenges. In this chapter, we will review nuances of estate planning for solo agers and those with limited beneficiaries, offering guidance and strategies to ensure that your legacy is preserved, and your wishes are honored.

DYING INTESTATE WITH NO LEGAL BENEFICIARIES

Consider, for example, Jane, a 60-year-old woman who recently lost her husband and has no children. Jane has not created a will or an estate plan, and she passes away suddenly. Her assets would then be distributed according to her state's intestate laws. Since Jane has no spouse or children, her estate might be divided among her siblings or other relatives, depending on the specific regulations in her state.

Now, let's imagine that Jane had no living relatives at all. In this case, her assets would become subject to escheatment, which means they would become the property of the state. This outcome is far from ideal, as close friends or charitable organizations that Jane may have wanted to support will not receive any portion of her estate. Furthermore, the state may not manage Jane's assets in a way that aligns with her values or wishes.

For example, if Jane had created a will or established a trust, she could have chosen to leave her assets to close friends, her favorite charity, or even a scholarship fund for her alma mater. By doing so, Jane would have had control over her legacy, and her assets would have been used in a manner consistent with her values and desires.

ESTATE PLANNING WITHOUT BENEFICIARIES...?

Estate planning is paramount in financial stewardship, especially for individuals without offspring or direct heirs. It safeguards your assets and wealth, ensuring they are dispersed according to your directives after your demise. Without a comprehensive estate plan, your resources could fall into the hands of those you didn't intend to or even revert to state ownership. The subsequent discussion offers essential points for those without immediate heirs, plus strategies for devising a thorough estate plan.

One must acknowledge that the absence of children or heirs can complicate estate planning decisions. In such scenarios, individuals often grapple with deciding the beneficiaries of their wealth or appointing a proxy for decision-making. Financial consultants typically suggest focusing on personal interests and aligning them with charitable contributions to address this issue.

For example, a childless, retired teacher might opt to set up a foundation, offering scholarships to college-bound students from an underprivileged middle school where she previously taught. Such philanthropic initiatives allow individuals to cultivate a legacy resonating with their values and passions.

It is essential to review and update your estate plan regularly, approximately every three years or after significant life events. Relationships with people and charities may change over time, and your estate plan should reflect these changes to ensure your resources are distributed according to your latest wishes.

Don't forget about your pets.

Concerns about your pet's welfare after your demise are valid. Though you cannot bequeath money directly to a pet, several alternatives exist to assure their well-being. This discussion elucidates some of these choices and provides guidelines for ensuring your cherished pet's secure and joyful future.

Bequeath your pet and some funds to a trustworthy person in your will or living trust.

For instance, you might bequeath your dog and $5,000 to a close relative or friend, coupled with a letter outlining your dog's nutritional requirements, favorite pastimes, and preferred veterinary care provider.

Establish a Pet Trust.

For example, you could set up a trust, allocating $10,000 for your cat's care, with a trusted friend appointed as trustee. The trust document would contain instructions on how the funds should be utilized for your cat's care, including veterinary expenses, food, and grooming.

Participate in a non-profit organization's scheme.

Numerous non-profit schemes nationwide provide or locate homes for pets when their owners cannot care for them. Some of these organizations necessitate a donation (typically between $10,000 and $25,000) to ensure your pet is placed in a nurturing home for the remainder of their lives.

Euthanasia provisions in your will

Though you can include a provision in your will instructing your executor to euthanize your pet humanely, such directions may not always be executed as desired. Courts often invalidate such provisions, typically considering it against societal norms to unnecessarily destroy valuable property. However, if you believe this is the best course for your pet, you must articulate your rationale to potential intervenors, such as your executor, beneficiaries, and family members.

Unique Considerations for Solo Agers and Those with Limited Beneficiaries

Estate planning for individuals living alone or with few beneficiaries involves addressing several unique concerns, including:

a. Designating Trusted Decision-Makers: With no immediate family or limited beneficiaries, it becomes crucial to identify and appoint trusted individuals or institutions to manage your financial affairs and execute your estate plan.

b. Long-Term Care Planning: Solo agers must consider their potential long-term care needs and ensure that they have adequate financial resources and insurance coverage to meet these needs.

c. Charitable Giving: For those with limited beneficiaries, incorporating charitable giving into their estate plan can be a meaningful way to create a lasting impact and fulfill personal values.

d. Establishing a Support Network: Building and maintaining a support network of friends, neighbors, and professionals is essential to ensure that your personal, financial, and healthcare needs are met as you age.

Strategies for Estate Planning with Limited Beneficiaries

The following strategies can be employed to create a comprehensive and tailored estate plan for solo agers or those with limited beneficiaries:

a. Customized Wills and Trusts: Drafting a detailed will and establishing trusts can provide a clear roadmap for the distribution of your assets, including specific bequests to friends, charities, or other organizations.

b. Durable Power of Attorney: Appoint a trusted individual or institution as your agent through a power of attorney.

c. Advance Healthcare Directives:

d. Pet Trusts: For those with pets, establishing a pet trust can ensure that your furry companions are well-cared for after your passing.

Specific Examples of Estate Planning for Solo Agers

The following examples illustrate how individuals living alone or with limited beneficiaries can effectively plan their estates:

A widowed retiree with no children designated a close friend as the executor of her estate and the agent in her durable power of attorney, ensuring that her financial and legal affairs would be managed by someone she trusted.

A successful entrepreneur with few family members incorporated charitable giving into his estate plan, bequeathing a significant portion of his wealth to a foundation he established to support education and environmental causes.

An individual without close relatives created an advance healthcare directive, appointing a trusted friend as her healthcare agent and providing clear instructions regarding her preferred medical treatments and end-of-life care.

Estate Planning 101 Summary

This book has provided the tools and knowledge necessary to create the best possible estate plan suited to your unique needs. Let's recap the key takeaways from each chapter.

Part 1: Tangible Wealth

Chapter 1: Discipline Now or Chaos Later?

Estate planning is essential for avoiding chaos and confusion after your death. Start by deciding who you want to inherit your assets, appointing a trusted executor, and consulting with an estate planning attorney. The stories shared in this chapter illustrate the importance of discipline and organization in estate planning.

Chapter 2: Shielding & Sheltering Your Retirement Income

Plan for retirement by setting goals, creating a savings plan, evaluating your investment portfolio, managing debt, considering healthcare expenses, and developing a retirement income plan. Avoid common retirement mistakes and make adjustments to your plan as needed.

Chapter 3: Old Age & Incapacity

Consider establishing trust and addressing the need for court-appointed guardians, administrators, and physical support options.

Chapter 4: Protecting & Providing for Your Family

Prepare for your family's future by creating a will, understanding the probate process, and avoiding common mistakes in estate planning. Learn how to provide for minors, special needs children, and surviving spouses, as well as minimize taxes and create protective trusts.

Part 2: Non-Tangible Wealth

Chapter 5: Preserving Your Legacy & Life Lessons

Pass down your values, traditions, and ideas by writing them down, sharing them with family members, using technology, creating a legacy plan, and engaging in philanthropy.

Chapter 6: Leaving Your Mark

Contribute to your community and the world through charitable foundations, legacy giving, volunteer work, artistic or cultural contributions, and donating to community structures. Consider your social media and online presence as part of your legacy.

Part 3: Legacy

Chapter 7: Lawsuits and Legal Eagles

Choose the right attorney for your estate planning needs and prepare for potential issues such as divorce, family conflicts, and post-execution management of your estate.

Chapter 8: Step-by-Step Estate Planning Strategies

Implement strategies such as wealth management, asset protection, tax minimization, business succession planning, and structured investments to optimize your estate plan.

Chapter 9: The Single Life

Even without legal beneficiaries, estate planning remains crucial. Consider your pets and other non-traditional beneficiaries in your estate planning process.

In conclusion, estate planning is vital to securing your future and leaving a lasting legacy. By implementing the strategies and lessons shared in this book, you can take charge of your old age and beyond, ensuring that your wealth, assets, and incomes are distributed according to your wishes and providing a sense of calm and peace in your life.

If you would like assistance in crafting your plan, just call our office at 630.560.1500 or email us at team@owatax.com.

Lastly,

Thank you from the bottom of my heart for being part of this journey. Your interest is noted, and I am grateful for the opportunity to be of service

Let's continue spreading the knowledge and empowering others through estate planning!

Wishing you the very best!

Dr. Darryl Franklin,

January 2024

PS - Sharing is caring! If you believe this book can benefit someone you know, consider passing it along. Together, we can create a ripple effect of positive change. You can also help by leaving a book review. Simply scan the code,

Or go to, https://notaxs.me/101 and leave your thoughts…

SPEAKER AVAILABILITY

Dr. Franklin also shares his passion for serving others in their personal development as he shares his unique life experiences as a keynote speaker and lecturer. Dr. Franklin's unique brand of academics, real-world experience, and humor provide a powerful alternative for your next event.

Topics Available:

Leadership,

Lifestyle,

Spirituality,

Marriage & Money,

Stewardship

The keynote presentations of Dr. Franklin are designed to fit the content and time considerations of your agenda with running times from 30 to 90 minutes.

Keynote Presentations:

Live Your Ideal Life

Four Keys To The Life Puzzle

How to Live An Extraordinary Life On Budget

Secrets To A Successful & Comfortable Lifestyle

How to Make Every Day A Payday!

To hire Dr. Franklin, phone 630-560-1500 or email team@owatax.com

ABOUT THE AUTHOR

Darryl Franklin graduated from the Illinois Institute of Technology with a Bachelor's Degree in Computer Science and completed graduate work at Northwestern University.

In 2001 a health-related miracle occurred. It was a life-changing event that caused the direction of his life to change. Searching for answers, Darryl returned to the Northwestern campus, earning a Masters Degree in Divinity from Garrett-Theological Evangelical Seminary. Concurrently, he became an ordained minister. Still not finding the answers to what was yearning within him, he continued, earning a Doctor of Philosophy from Benedictine University. It was in the writing of his dissertation that some of the answers to the life puzzle began to emerge.

Today, Dr. Franklin is CEO of Oakwood Wealth Advisors and Tax Office where his team "helps clients get their entire financial house in order." Dr. Franklin served as a Faculty Lecturer at Benedictine University where he taught MBA622-*Creativity and Innovation in Business,* MBA653-*Investment Theory & Portfolio Management*, and MBA656-*Investment Analysis.*

Committed to the community and education, Dr. Franklin also serves in the local church as a staff minister. He is currently the Chairman of the Board of Garrett-Evangelical Theological Seminary and is a former local School District Board member.

REFERENCES

Atlanta GA Estate Planning Blog. A. A. (2023, August 16). Charitable Giving in Your Estate Plan: How It Works for GA Residents. Atlanta GA Estate Planning Blog. https://www.atlantagaestateplanning.com/blog/2023/08/16/charitable-giving-in-your-estate-plan-how-it-works-for-ga-residents/

Attorneys Real Estate Group. (n.d.). Living Will vs. Power of Attorney. AttorneysRE. https://attorneysre.com/living-will-vs-power-of-attorney/

Charitable Giving In Your Estate Plan: How It Works For GA Residents - Brian Douglas Law. https://www.atlantagaestateplanning.com/blog/2023/08/16/charitable-giving-in-your-estate-plan-how-it-works-for-ga-residents/

Dana Law Group. (n.d.). Maximizing Tax Benefits Through Estate Planning in Arizona. Dana Law Group. https://danalawgroup.com/maximizing-tax-benefits-through-estate-planning-in-arizona/

ElderWell Franchise. (n.d.) The Impact of Dementia on Caregivers & Loved Ones. ElderWell Franchise. https://elderwellfranchise.com/the-impact-of-dementia-on-caregivers-loved-ones/

Estate Law Partners. (n.d.). How a Revocable Living Trust Works. Estate Law Partners. https://www.estatelawpartners.com/estate-planning/how-a-revocable-living-trust-works/

Finance Training Topics. (n.d.). Power of Attorney Helps With Estate Planning. Finance Training Topics. https://financetrainingtopics.net/power-of-attorney-helps-with-estate-planning/

Hernandez, M. S. (2014). *Breaking the Silence: My Final Forty Days as a Public School Teacher.* ISBN 1626529620.

Illinois Lawyer Now. A. A. (2023, September). Three Ways a Special Needs Trust May Benefit Your Family. Illinois Lawyer Now. https://www.illinoislawyernow.com/2023/09/three-ways-a-special-needs-trust-may-benefit-your-family/

Jones, T. (n.d.). Living Will. DrTimJones.com. https://drtimjones.com/living-will/

San Diego Foundation. (n.d.). How to Start a Private Foundation. San Diego Foundation. https://www.sdfoundation.org/news-events/sdf-news/how-to-start-a-private-foundation/

Slonim Law. (n.d.). Estate Planning Attorney in Melbourne, FL. Slonim Law. https://slonimlaw.com/estate-planning-attorney-melbourne-fl/

The Business Finance. (n.d.). Retirement Mistakes to Avoid. The Business Finance. https://thebusinessfinance.net/retirement-mistakes-to-avoid/

The Reading League. (n.d.). Planned Giving. The Reading League. https://www.thereadingleague.org/donate/planned-giving/

Touchstone Publishers. (n.d.). The Importance of Leaving a Legacy and How You Can Do It by Example. Touchstone Publishers. https://touchstonepublishers.com/the-importance-of-leaving-a-legacy-and-how-you-can-do-it-by-example/

Verywell Health. (n.d.). How to Start a Patient Advocates Business. Verywell Health. https://www.verywellhealth.com/how-to-start-a-patient-advocates-business-2614916

Made in the USA
Las Vegas, NV
06 November 2025

33813699R00116